a camel named joe

A
CAMEL NAMED
JOE

THE ILLUSTRATED STORY

OF AN AMERICAN

POP ICON

DAVID DeSMITH

duCap
BOOKS

Published in 1998 by
duCap Books
Boston, MA

ISBN *0-9665006-0-1 (hardbound)*

This book was produced for adult smokers 21 years of age or older.
It was distributed through the age-restricted
Camel Cash Timeless Collectibles Catalog.

First Edition
Printed and bound in the United States of America

"Self Portrait," 1992

For Joe Camel, wherever he is.

FOREWORD

In the ten years since he first slipped into a pair of shades, Joe Camel served as a lightning rod for anti-smoking activists, a rallying cry for free-speech advocates, and the central image for one of the most successful advertising campaigns of all time. You can look it up. But not here.

This isn't a book about politics. This is, quite simply, a book about Joe, a charismatic camel who became nothing less than an American pop phenomenon.

Joe got mail, lots of it — even a wedding invitation once. Apocryphal accounts have him getting more local write-in votes than certain third-party candidates. In a particularly telling example of just how real he became in the American popular imagination, a New York City focus group of racially diverse 20-somethings spontaneously got into a heated debate about whether Joe was black or white. Joe struck a chord for racial harmony that day when they finally agreed that he was, after all, just a very cool camel and, consequently, belonged to everybody.

As one of the creative types who was around from nearly the beginning, I can tell you it wasn't just the campaign's audience who saw Joe as something more than just a fantasy. During one of the occasional agency-client tugs o' war over creative execution, our side volleyed, only half-jokingly, "But we don't work for you. We work for Joe."

Sooner or later, everyone who worked on the campaign ended up with a little Joe Camel in him. Or her. Then again, we knew there was something at the heart of Joe's character that was quintessentially American, so maybe he was there all along.

As you flip through the pages of this book, there is only one rule of thumb — have some fun with it. We sure did.

— JOHN MEZZINA
CHAIRMAN, EXECUTIVE CREATIVE DIRECTOR
MEZZINA/BROWN, INC.

ix

INTRODUCTION

The year was 1987 and Camel was going to be 75 years old in 1988. That was when we decided to throw the biggest birthday party in advertising history. The problem was, we needed a big idea for the birthday celebration and we had only six months to turn this idea into a full-blown promotion. This is the story of how we threw a heck of a birthday party . . . and created the ultimate spokescamel in the process.

We started with a look at the history of the brand. First, Camel had a rich heritage and was well known for its marketing savvy. Not only was it the first nationally marketed cigarette brand in America, but it was also launched with the first ever teaser advertising campaign. The ads ran in newspapers all over the country announcing "The Camels Are Coming!" and, not knowing the brand, people pictured herds of camels running through their neighborhoods. This campaign created a lot of excitement around the new brand, and Camel soon became America's number-one selling cigarette. In addition, the 1920's slogan, "I'd Walk A Mile For A Camel," became so popular that you can still hear people mention it today. So, let's just say that we had some pretty big shoes to fill.

Enter Joe Camel. But first, a little background.

We were working with several ad agencies who were given the assignment to create a huge 75th birthday party for Camel. We told them to make sure that whatever was created would modernize the brand. We also thought that maybe it was time to develop a new spokesperson. So we said to the agencies: "Imagine a guy who's fun, exciting, and in touch with all kinds of adult smokers." We even gave them a poster from France in which an artist had created a bust of a camel's face. He had big brown eyes, a prominent nose, and human ears. The agencies created several concepts that were tested among adult smokers, including this Camel "guy". This Camel "guy" won hands down — they thought he was great.

Now, of course, when you create a fictitious camel and give him human characteristics, you get into all kinds of weird discussions. How many fingers should he have? What color should his eyes be? And then, finally, we realized that we were creating our own spokesperson and we could make him however we wanted. Eventually, we settled on 4 fingers, no toes (we thought they would never be shown), and beautiful, charming blue eyes.

And then there was his name. We wanted to make our camel guy very intriguing but, at the same time, an average kind of guy who could relate to adult smokers of all kinds — picture everybody's favorite bartender at the local bar. The name "Joe" seemed to fit that description, but we were still debating. Then, we were reminded that the camel graphic on our packs was inspired by a 1913 photograph of a circus camel named "Ol' Joe." That settled it. Joe it was. And his last name? Camel — what else? We had our spokescamel.

Now we needed to do a little party planning. As we said before, we wanted to do something innovative and exciting . . . something that no one in marketing had ever done before. We also wanted to give Camel smokers a reason to celebrate. You see, Camel smokers are a special breed — they go for what's unique and adventurous. So the party was for our brand and its adult smokers . . . because they deserved it.

The first big idea we had was to develop a magazine ad that sang "Happy Birthday." We knew this would stop adult smokers in their tracks because singing print ads just weren't done back then. Unfortunately, everyone thought we'd lost our minds. Supplier after supplier came in to meet with us, only to deliver the bad news that this couldn't be done . . . it was impossible. After long hours of meetings, we worked out all of the logistics and figured out that it could be done. But would our management let us? Time would tell.

Of course, one singing ad does not a birthday party make. So we looked at all the parts of the marketing mix to see just how fun and unexpected we could make this whole event. One thing was for sure — a birthday party's not much of a party without presents. So we decided to put a few premium items in retail stores — a 75th-birthday mug, an autoshade, and some playing cards — which were given away free when adult smokers bought packs of Camel.

For billboards, we wanted to announce our new slogan "75 Years and Still Smokin'" with Joe and pyramids lit up like spotlights. We found a supplier who could line our billboards with high-tech gold-spangled sheets to give us the impact we wanted. Things were coming together.

The last thing, of course, was the party itself. We planned a huge event in Los Angeles that would bring the whole world of Camel to life: we planned to build pyramids, have belly dancers, the works. But the big hit of the evening was to be the live camel races. It was definitely going to be quite a party.

Now that we had our plans finalized, we had to do some final testing to make certain that this was the right thing to do. First, we went to the factory floors — to talk to the people who made the Camel product. Then we went to focus groups and talked to lots of adult Camel smokers. And, just as we thought, Joe was loved by adult smokers from all walks of life. Almost everyone who saw this fun-loving, adventurous camel named Joe loved him immediately and they said that he was the perfect "spokesperson" for their brand. He brought laughter and excitement back into the world of Camel, something that had been missing for a long time.

Finally, we were ready for launch. And then, just a short time before everything was about to hit the marketplace, someone important decided that he did not like our choice of eye color. He said: "Camels have brown eyes so why shouldn't this camel have brown eyes too?" We explained to him that he was our creation so he could have any eye color we chose. But he was adamant. We explained to him how much money this was going to cost the company to change the eye color at this late date. He didn't budge. So, at the last minute, Joe had to have eye surgery and, sure enough, his eyes were changed to brown.

In the end, Camel had its big birthday party just the way we planned it and, from all accounts, everything was a huge success, especially the ad that sang "Happy Birthday." It only ran in one magazine, but that ad created so much excitement, newsstands sold out in no time. As for the billboards, rumor has it that they stopped traffic in several cities. And the retail presents? They were a smash hit. So, amid a flurry of celebration and excitement, Joe emerged in style . . . just the way you'd expect him to.

So that's it. Now you know the real story of the early days behind Joe Camel. And, as you look through this book, take a look at Joe's eyes. You see, somewhere along the way, we, too, became important people and, as you know, we were always kind of partial to our blue-eyed Joe.

—Lynn Beasley

Executive Vice-President of Marketing

R.J. Reynolds Tobacco Co.

—Fran Creighton

Vice-President Marketing, Camel Brand

R.J. Reynolds Tobacco Co.

PREFACE

The advertising art shown in this book is the work of many people. Copywriters and art directors who conceived of the situations. Sketch artists who did initial pencil drawings. A small group of other artists who did the actual paintings. Retouchers who put the finishing touches on each execution. Production people who ensured that the artwork was properly reproduced for publication. And a host of other behind-the-scenes workers — from account executives to the clients at Camel — without whose guidance, support and tenacity these ads might never have seen the light of day.

In most cases, the artwork represented in the book is finished art, paintings that were taken through the entire production process and ran as ads in magazines or on billboards much as they are shown here. In some cases, though, the artwork is "comp" art, unfinished ad concepts that are shown for the most part as colored, watercolor marker drawings. Since many of these ideas were offbeat, or came with interesting stories attached, it seemed worthwhile to include them even though they are a bit rougher than the finished pieces of art.

The book contains over 250 pieces of art in all. And while a chapter could probably be written about each one, the text has instead been kept to a minimum. This is, first and foremost, an art book: a visual chronicle of Joe Camel and the ad campaign in which he appeared.

Often, Camel solicited comments and opinions about the ads it was considering. Smokers who were 21 and over were invited to participate in panel discussions called "focus groups." This opinion research helped the brand team determine which ideas were good ones, and which should be jettisoned. Where focus groups are mentioned in this book, it is these discussion groups that are being referred to.

Between 1988 and 1997, the Joe Camel campaign was one of the most recognized ad campaigns in America, and that was due largely to its fans, devotees of Joe who appreciated the wit and irreverence he personified. If you number yourself among those, this book was really created for you. Here's hoping you enjoy it.

— DAVID DESMITH

"Singing Insert," 1988

"Pyramid Pop-Up," 1988

He didn't throw a coin across any major American rivers. He didn't engineer a new operating system and make zillions in the computer market. He didn't even bat .400 or win the Triple Crown. He simply crashed a party. But by the time the festivities ended nine years later, he'd become one of the most recognizable figures in America. Without ever uttering a word.

From day one, Joe Camel had what it took to get smoker's attention. In the first place, he wasn't just smoking Camels — he was a smoking camel. He was a visual pun, an updating of the brand that had made *Camelus Dromedarius* its trademark decades before. But he was far from just an ordinary camel. Because like so many

FREE Pack of Camels!
When You Buy 1. Any Style. (Coupon On Back)

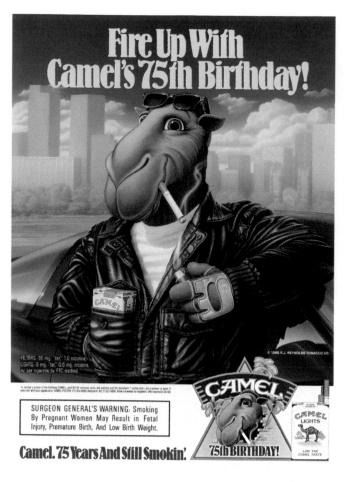

"Fire Up," 1988

"Catch It," 1988

other mythological figures before him, Joe was a creature endowed with certain human characteristics—characteristics which, in his case, went well beyond the ability to enjoy an occasional smoke.

Joe could do things that most of us only dream of. And he was always up to something new. One day you'd see him popping open a bottle of champagne in celebration of a victory at the race track. The next day he'd be casting for trout in some picturesque mountain stream. His lifestyle was an enjoyable one—and it was not subject to compromise.

The word "irreverent" is frequently used to describe the Joe Camel campaign, and a look

at its introductory ads shows why. Beyond the use of an illustrated smoking camel, beyond the strident colors and cheeky graphic design, there was an inherent political-incorrectness to the whole idea. "75 Years and Still Smokin" was more than just a birthday message. It was a statement about attitude—something there was no shortage of once Joe hit the scene.

From the start, there was a whimsical quality to the Joe campaign, an innate sense of humor that made it stand out in its category like a black sheep on a hillside of driven snow. Far from the macho seriousness of the long-running Marlboro ad campaign, and farther still from the silliness of the "Happy Models Smoking" imagery other

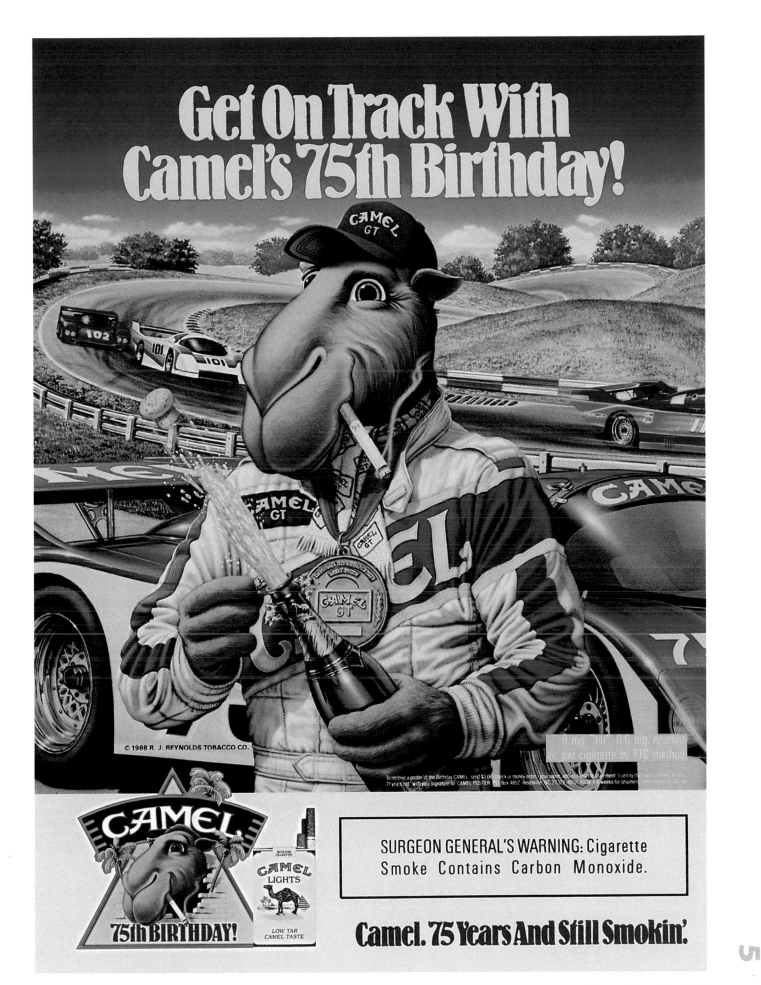

"Get on Track," 1988

Joe Camel brought back memories of the brand's trademark dromedary. While the Camel packaging, which hearkened back to its 1913 roots, provided a classic link to the past, it was Joe's appearance on the scene that gave the brand's packaging new relevance and kept it from seeming old-fashioned.

brands fell back on, the Joe Camel campaign was droll. It was imaginative. It was tongue-in-cheek. And farcical. It ran the risk of being noticed. Which is why, to this day, people will still tell you about the campaign's introductory insert, which played *Happy Birthday* on a sound chip when you opened it up.

Joe Camel changed the face of cigarette advertising. And he did it with a grin.

The campaign itself celebrated nine more birthdays before it was retired toward the end of 1997. And along the way, Joe made more friends (and enemies) than Hollywood and Washington combined. What had begun as a short-term, birthday-party promotion just kept going and going. What sustained it, and kept Joe alive for so long in America's popular imagination, is what the rest of this book is about.

The very first Joe Camel T-shirt, the "75th Anniversary T-shirt," 1988.
Today, it's quite a collector's item.

"The Wild Pack," 1988. This was the first ad which revealed the "Camel Guy's" name to be Joe.

eWild Pack!
20 FILTER CIGARETTES
CAMEL
FILTERS
SMOOTH
TURKISH & DOMESTIC
BLEND
CAMEL FILTERS
LIGHTS: 9 mg. "tar", 0.6 mg. nicotine,
FILTERS: 16 mg. "tar", 1.0 mg. nicotine,
av. per cigarette by FTC method.
Joe
© 1988 R.J. REYNOLDS TOBACCO CO.

"Submarine," 1989

> " JOE WAS LARGER THAN
LIFE FROM THE VERY
BEGINNING. "

2

ONE SMOOTH
CHARACTER

"High Roller," 1989

People have used lots of different adjectives to describe Joe Camel over the years, not all of them complimentary. One which was used a lot, especially in the campaign's early going, was "smooth."

The "Smooth Character" era, which began in 1989, saw Joe Camel develop from an oddity, a promotional novelty, into an advertising symbol with a well-defined personality. All the attributes that people ascribed to Joe throughout his years as Camel's front man had their roots in his early days as Mr. Smooth Character.

Joe was larger than life from the very beginning. He rendezvoused with submarines, basked in the California sun, rolled the bones in Vegas, and then just for kicks, rolled up his french-cuffed sleeves to shoot a little eight-ball. And whatever Joe did, he did with flair. So it's no wonder he earned so much attention. And admiration.

"GT Racer," 1989

"Hollywood" 1989

"High Flyer" 1989

Matchbooks like the one shown here were an important part of Camel's marketing mix. Hundreds of different ones were developed during Joe's reign and each one reflected a different side of Joe's personality and his world.

In his Smooth Character days, Joe was portrayed as a real guy's guy. He did "manly" things—and women always took notice of him. In fact, each of the hyper-colorful ads in this series would be easy to distinguish from the ones that followed it even without the copy. Because in every situation, regardless of what Joe was doing, there was a female (a human one, that is) watching him from afar.

One ad even went a step further. In the 1989 ad called "Billiard Room," not only was there a

blonde looking over her shoulder at Joe, there was also a guy off in the distance who was being ignored by the woman. This, of course, may have raised an issue for men who came across this ad. Should they identify with Joe, the camel with a style all his own? Or were they represented in the scene by the forgotten guy in the background? The ad sent mixed signals, and a lesson was learned: don't destroy the fantasy by imposing too much reality.

By the end of 1989, this series of ads had helped define Joe's personality in a way that would stick for years. An illustrated, mythological world had been created—a world in which all things were do-able. And the multi-talented character at the center of that world had opened a big door for the Camel brand.

Free with a two-pack purchase, this hat enabled any average adult smoker to don a piece of Joe's world.

Thank you for ordering

The Illustrated History of Joe.

A copy of this special, authorized biography has been reserved for you, and will be delivered as soon as it rolls off the presses.

With over 200 glossy pages, this special, hard-cover edition features Joe's most unforgettable moments over a ten-year span. And with an early fall release, you'll be one of the first to recapture the years that made Joe famous. This is one story that is worth the wait.

If the book does not arrive by November 1, 1998, please call 1-800-926-8814.

"Billiard Room," 1989

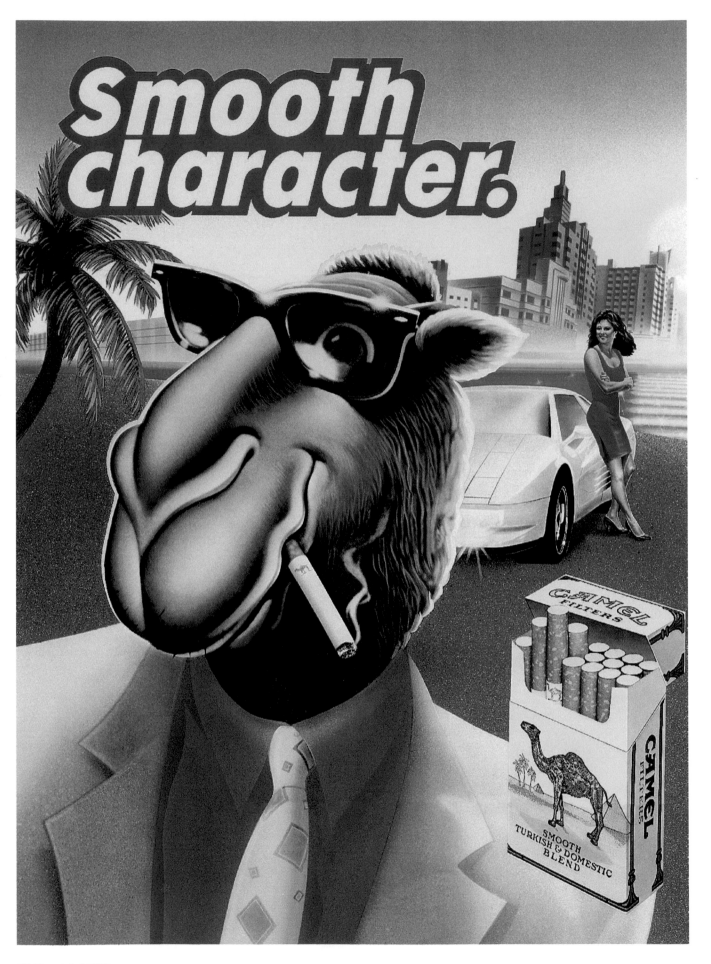

"Miami," 1989

The campaign went bilingual with ads like these 1989 executions which ran in Miami, New York, Los Angeles, and other markets in the southwestern U.S.

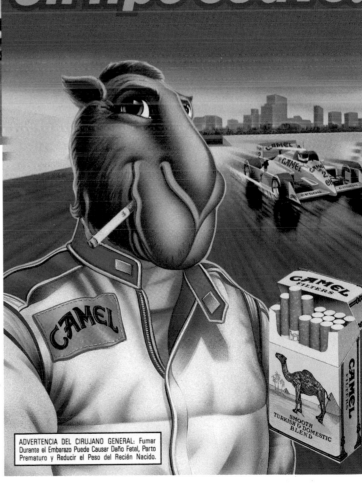

"Piano Player," 1990

> "IN THESE ADS, SMOOTH CHARACTER
> BECAME MORE OF AN
> AVERAGE JOE."

3

A CAMPAIGN
WITH LEGS

"Après Ski," 1990

"Water Skiing," 1990

As Joe became more and more popular, finding new and different ways to portray him became the campaign's chief challenge. So it was that Joe, after a couple of solid years of appearing as just a bust, finally got to make use of all his appendages.

Previous ads had established Joe as an uncommon sort of camel. Meeting submarines in your tuxedo is, after all, not your everyday leisure activity. But as the Joe campaign evolved, there was less and less need to portray him in that manner. The fact that he was a smoking camel was fantastic enough — he didn't need to go to the moon to get attention.

In fact, one ad in which Joe became a lunar explorer was actually mocked up and tested. The reaction? "Whoa! He can't do that! — he's a camel!" It was okay

for Joe to light up, drive fast cars, and engage in other popular leisure activities as long as they were of this Earth. But too much fantasy apparently destroyed the fun that was inherent in Joe's mimicry of human endeavors.

For the people working on the campaign, this revelation was a liberating one. Because to them, Joe had never really been the larger-than-life figure he'd sometimes been portrayed as. He was more like a good buddy, someone you saw every day at work and always got along with. And now, smokers evidently saw him that way, too.

In these ads, Smooth Character became more of an average Joe. He did the things we all do (or would like to do) and in some

"Canoe," 1990

executions, like *Tux Torso*, even did nothing at all while still delivering a brand message with attitude.

But as Joe acquired arms and legs, and was shown from new and different perspectives, one question came up. Does Joe, like his four-legged camel cousins, have a tail? It's a question that remains unanswered to this day.

"Sailing," 1990

"Tux Torso," 1990

"Downtown Smooth," 1990

"Bus Stop," 1992

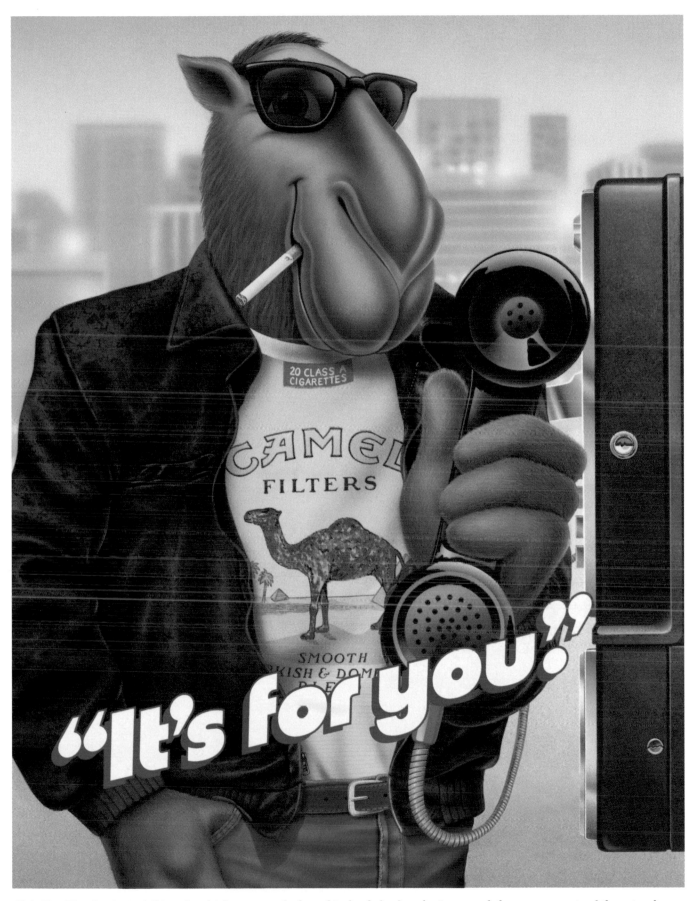

"It's For You," 1990. This ad, which ran on telephone kiosks, helped make Joe one of the most recognized faces in the land. In 1990, New York City in particular saw a lot of Joe. Subways, bus stops, phone booths, billboards — Joe got around.

"Hot Tub," 1991

"Motorcycle," 1990

"Sports Car," 1991

"Have You Seen This Camel?"

Joe had style. And with their own Joe watch, adult Camel smokers were free to arrive fashionably late—or early.

"Golf," 1991

THE PREMIER OF

Smooth

CAMEL ADVERTISING SUPPLEMENT

CHARACTER OF THE YEAR

Front cover of Smooth Magazine, *1990*

JOE CAMEL
Ambassador of Smooth

"AS A COLORFUL PARODY OF CELEBRITY MAGAZINES . . .

SMOOTH MAGAZINE WAS A GAS. AS A VEHICLE

FOR DIMENSIONALIZING JOE'S PERSONALITY,

IT WAS HIGH OCTANE."

4

COVER
GUY

"Midnight at the Oasis," 1990

Whatever you called him—whether it was Joe Camel, Smooth Character, Joe Smooth, or just the Camel Guy—chances are you saw plenty of him in your favorite magazines. Between 1988 when the campaign was launched and 1997 when it was discontinued, Joe appeared in issue after issue of America's most highly read magazines among adults. From *People* and *GQ* to *Bassmaster* and *Soap Opera Digest,* Joe showed his face in more than 125 different publications. But for the people marketing the Camel brand, Joe was not the kind of guy who did anything half-way. "He ought to be on a cover," they said. "Better yet, he ought to have his *own* magazine."

And thus, *Smooth* was born.

Smooth ran as a magazine insert—in other words, as a mini-magazine that showed up inside the magazine you were reading. And it was seen as the perfect vehicle for bringing the expanding and evolving world of Joe Camel to life. From cover to cover, it was a no-holds-barred celebration of all things Joe. Inside were features like "Joe's Smooth Philosophies," which offered Joe's special brand of irreverent wisdom. Joe's Smooth Philosophy on In Laws, for example, said: "What's the difference between in-laws and outlaws? Outlaws are wanted."

"Midnight at the Oasis," another feature of the first *Smooth,* depicted a party scene in which camels from all walks of life were gathered in their favorite neighborhood bar. All of Joe's buddies were in attendance, but a camel-wannabe cowboy was unceremoniously denied entry.

At eight pages, *Smooth* was many times more impactful than your average single-page magazine ad. It was also many times more expensive to produce and run. Nonetheless, a second *Smooth* was created with the intention of distributing it four months after the first. It, too, included a party scene — with the requisite joke being played on yet another poor cowboy — and several tongue-in-cheek movie-related features, including reviews of Joe's performances in the smash hits: "A Midwinter Lights Dream" and "ReQuest For Fire."

Due to fiscal obstacles, the second *Smooth* never ran. But some of the art which was created for that issue did subsequently make its way into a Camel matchbook series, showing Joe in other starring roles such as "Dr. Jekyll and Mr. Smooth," and "The Incredible 50-Foot Camel."

As a colorful parody of magazines, their features, and the celebrities they covetously pursue, *Smooth Magazine* was a gas. As a vehicle for dimensionalizing Joe's personality, it was high octane. *Smooth* put Smooth Character in a class by himself. Because after all, as any celebrity will tell you, you haven't really made it until you've gotten your first cover.

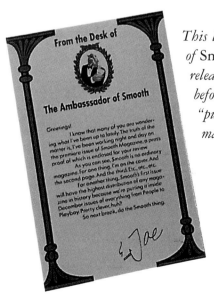

This letter accompanied copies of Smooth *which were released to the press just before its initial "publication" inside of other major magazines.*

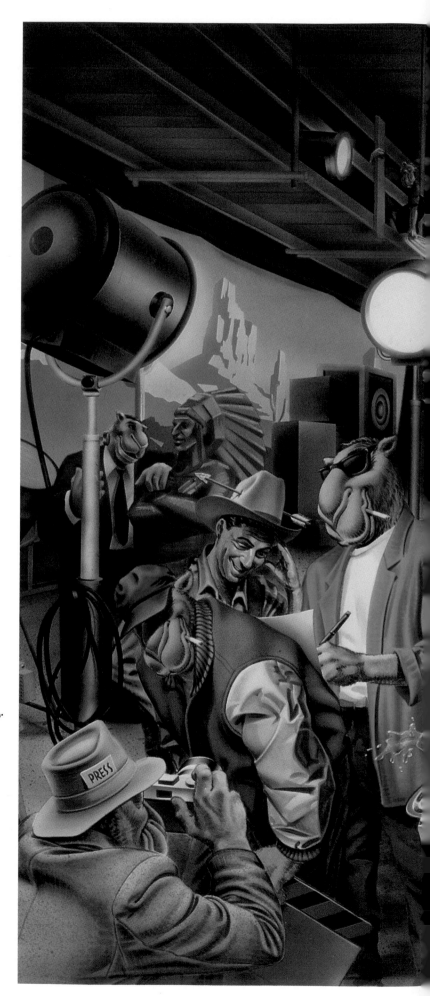

"Cast Party," 1991

MONUMENT

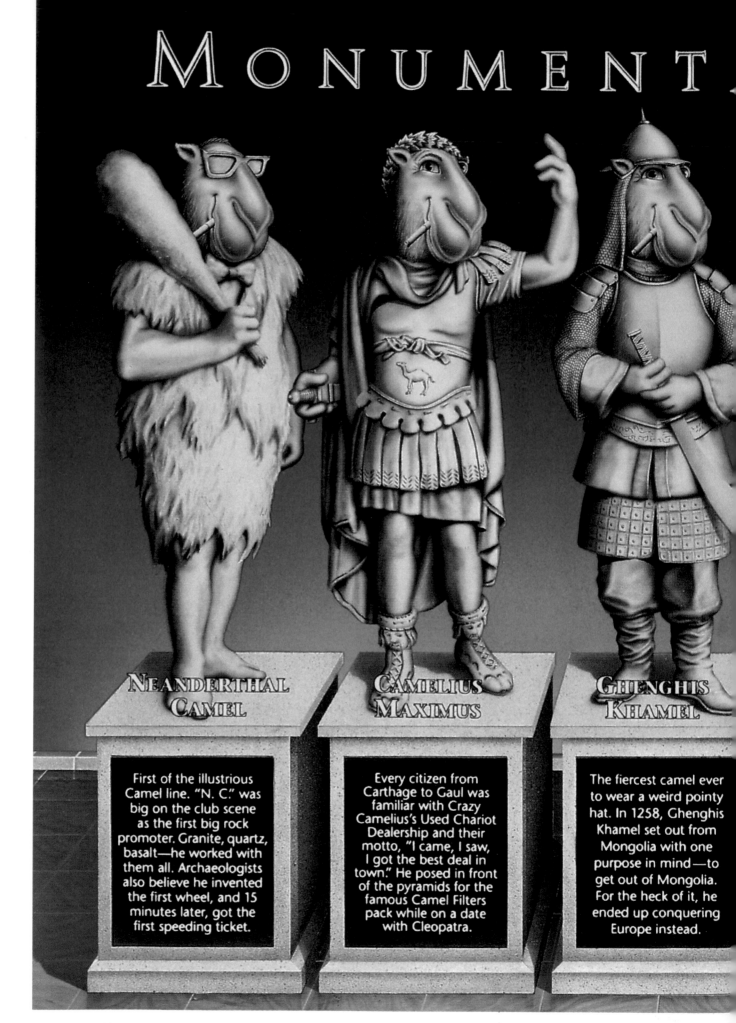

NEANDERTHAL CAMEL

First of the illustrious Camel line. "N. C." was big on the club scene as the first big rock promoter. Granite, quartz, basalt—he worked with them all. Archaeologists also believe he invented the first wheel, and 15 minutes later, got the first speeding ticket.

CAMELIUS MAXIMUS

Every citizen from Carthage to Gaul was familiar with Crazy Camelius's Used Chariot Dealership and their motto, "I came, I saw, I got the best deal in town." He posed in front of the pyramids for the famous Camel Filters pack while on a date with Cleopatra.

GHENGHIS KHAMEL

The fiercest camel ever to wear a weird pointy hat. In 1258, Ghenghis Khamel set out from Mongolia with one purpose in mind—to get out of Mongolia. For the heck of it, he ended up conquering Europe instead.

"Monumentally Smooth," 1990

SIR JOSEPH OF CAMELOT

There wasn't enough room for him to sit at King Arthur's Round Table, so Sir Joseph had to sit at a card table in the basement. However, Sir Joseph was renowned for his bravery, having once turned a fire-breathing dragon into the first disposable lighter.

LEONARDO DA CAMEL

Owner of Leonardo's 1-Hour Portraits, he became the subject of scandal when it was revealed that his masterpiece, the "Mona Lisa," was crafted from a paint-by-numbers kit. In his own defense he said: "Hey, at least I stayed within the lines!"

STONEWALL CAMEL

The top of his class at West Point, Stonewall cut a dashing and unusual figure as a camel riding a horse. Not wishing to offend either the North or the South during the Civil War, he decided to fight for the West. He never lost a battle.

"The Incredible 50-Foot Camel," 1991

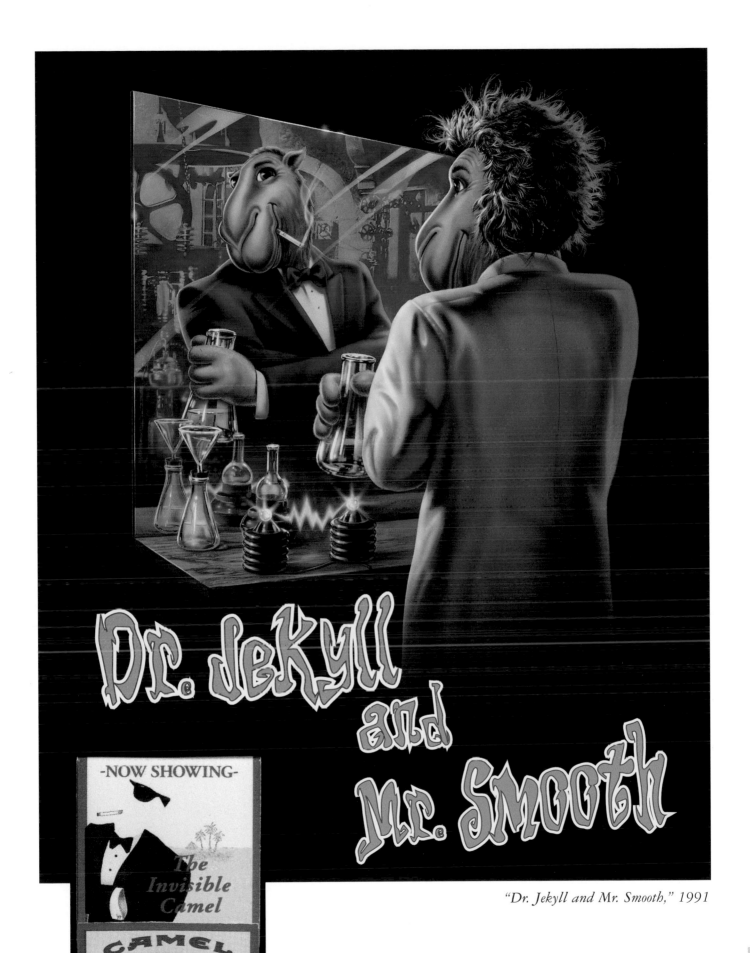

"Dr. Jekyll and Mr. Smooth," 1991

Movie Poster matchbook: "The Invisible Camel"

"Neon Joe," 1990

Neon signals excitement, action.
It's shorthand for "check me out."
In other words, it was the

perfect look for joe.

5

JOE GOES
ULTRA

"Ultras," 1990

"They're Coming," 1990.
This "teaser" ad was posted
a month before Camel's new
Ultra Lights cigarettes hit
the shelves in stores.

eon is as much a part of the American landscape as flags on the Fourth of July. In fact, even then, you're liable to see more neon signs than flags—and some of those signs will probably mimic Old Glory. Neon signals excitement, action. It's shorthand for "Check me out."

In other words, it was the perfect look for Joe.

By the Spring of 1990, Joe Camel was well enough known that even in neon, there was no mistaking him for anybody else. And as Camel looked for a way to introduce its new Ultra Lights style, using illustrations which depicted a "Neon Joe" proved to be a pretty bright idea.

Neon was the "ultra" look for the ultra Camel, and it yielded twin benefits. In the first place, the ads felt introductory — they shouted that there was news. It was a new look for Joe and a new look for Camel. Secondly, Neon Joe didn't

THEY'RE COMING

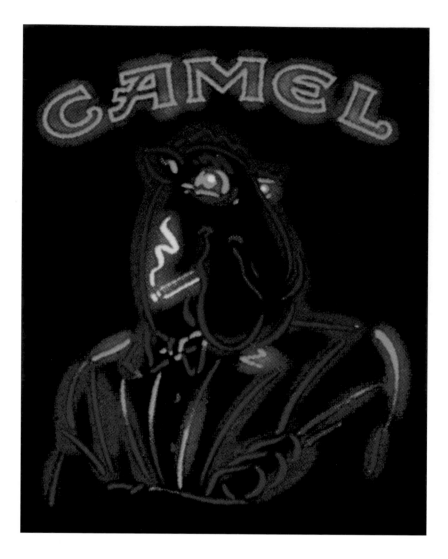

The perfect promotional item for Camel's Ultra Lights launch? A neon sign, naturally.

overpower the message as a full-color illustration of Joe might have. The new pack stood out in the ads, which was a good thing. Because in this case — unlike previous Joe ads — the pack was more important than the character. There was a new product to sell.

Back then, it was an ironic fact that the more Camel screamed "Smooth," the more there was a need for a smoother, lighter style in the Camel product lineup. Camel Ultra Lights, the thinking went, would give Lights smokers the Camel they were looking for — a cigarette that would deliver, quote: the rich taste of Camel's traditional Turkish and Domestic Blend, with more smoothness than other Camels, unquote.

The Neon Joe campaign for Ultra Lights generated a lot of excitement — and a lot of trial. And while Ultra Lights didn't instantly become Camel's biggest style, they did earn a small but loyal following that's still around to this day — long after all the neon signs picturing Joe have come down.

"20 Ultra Lights," matchbook

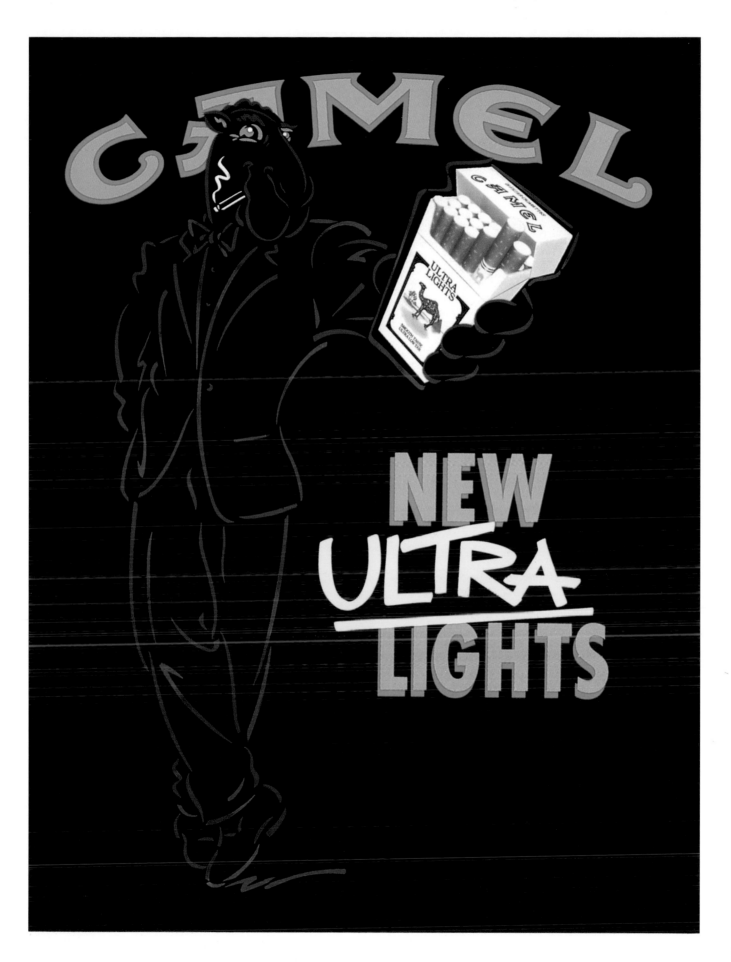

"New Ultra Lights," 1990

"The Hard Pack," 1991
This ad, which was designed and illustrated in an album-cover style, added four new characters to Joe's world.

JOE WAS IN DANGER OF BECOMING

THE WORLD'S LONELIEST CAMEL. THE

HARD PACK CHANGED ALL THAT."

6

T H E

HARD PACK

"Hard Pack II," 1991

erek had the Dominoes. Gladys Knight had the Pips. Tom Petty had the Heartbreakers. And The Captain had Tenille — or was it the other way around? In the pantheon of modern music, the frontliner and the backup band are as old a convention as the two-step. Each helped define the other; the sum of the parts was greater than the whole.

For Joe, though, The Hard Pack provided more than just musical accompaniment. They introduced an element of sociability to the campaign that was otherwise lacking. After three years of basically going it on his own, Joe was in danger of becoming the world's loneliest camel. The Hard Pack changed all that — although that wasn't the sole reason they were created.

In early 1991, the trend in cigarette sales was toward boxed products (as opposed to soft packs). Marlboro, with its "Flip-Top Box," owned the lion's share of the market. Many people didn't even know that Camel offered a boxed product. "That," said the people at R.J. Reynolds, "is something we need to change."

But how?

The answer was right there all along — printed on the bottom of every box of Camels. For Camel didn't call its boxes "boxes." It called them "Hard Packs."

Bingo — The Hard Pack was born. But the troupe wasn't originally a blues band. In its earliest incarnation it was just a group of Joe's buddies. Only after focus groups revealed concerns about the rough-and-tumble appearance of the

"Hard Pack III," 1991

new characters did they become a band with instruments. Then smokers began to sing a different tune.

The Hard Pack: four unique individuals, each with his own style, his own instrument, and his own preferred kind of Camel cigarettes. There was Bustah on guitar and Hard Pack Lights, Eddie on drums and Hard Pack 99's, Floyd on sax and Hard Pack Ultra Lights, and Max on harmonica and Hard Pack Filters. They were both like Joe and unlike Joe, and over the course of the years between 1991 and 1997, they took the Joe campaign to new and different places.

The Hard Pack went on a U.S. tour — a sojourn chronicled in ads as well as on a series of Camel matchbooks. They joined Joe at Club Camel, where their smooth sound mingled with that of the surf to create just the right atmosphere. They helped introduce Camel 99's — Camel's irreverent take on 100 millimeter cigarettes. And they graced the sides of several zillion lighters.

The Hard Pack brought a new dimension of congeniality to the campaign. They hung out in diners together. They shot pool together. They got haircuts together. They were social animals. They went where Joe couldn't necessarily go —

"Couch," 1991

"Pool Hall," 1992, *a design for a match tin.*

and did some things that Joe probably wouldn't do. Like showing up in kilts, for example.

Joe Camel didn't need the Hard Pack to be popular among adult smokers. But there's little doubt that what Eddie, Bustah, Floyd and Max brought to the campaign helped sustain it, and kept it going longer than it might have otherwise. For Joe, they were good friends to the end.

"Ringside," 1992

"Kilts," 1994

"Diner," 1992

"Mt. Rushmore," 1995

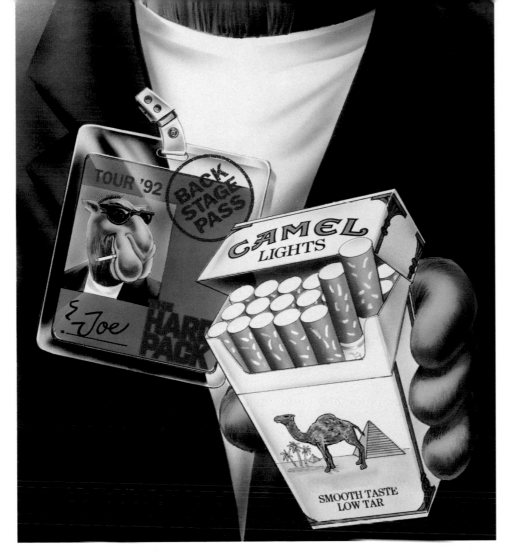

"Backstage Pass," 1994

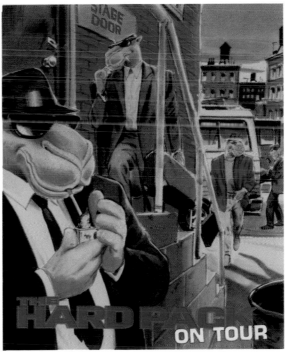

"Summer Tour," 1995

Above: The Hard Pack "Shore Tour" T-shirt was another example of how art from the campaign was used to support promotional events, in this case a T-shirt offer for East Coast beach towns.

THE HARD PACK LAYS DOWN SOME TRACKS

From the moment The Hard Pack was formed, it was inevitable that at some point they'd take a break from touring and record an album or two. They got their chance in 1993, when they holed up in a New Orleans studio for a couple of weeks. Shortly thereafter "Meet The Hard Pack" was released.

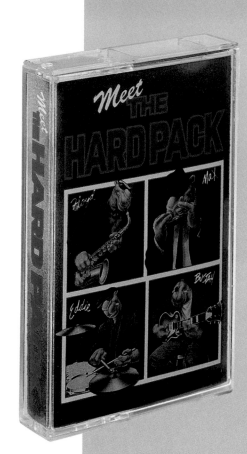

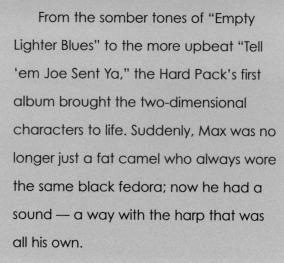

From the somber tones of "Empty Lighter Blues" to the more upbeat "Tell 'em Joe Sent Ya," the Hard Pack's first album brought the two-dimensional characters to life. Suddenly, Max was no longer just a fat camel who always wore the same black fedora; now he had a sound — a way with the harp that was all his own.

The songs were humorous, energetic, and even touching. They revealed a band with range — and talent.

In some cases, the songs worked to address specific tactical objectives for the Camel brand. "Don't Gimme No Cheap Cigarettes," for example, was specifically written to discourage Camel smokers from trading down to low-price, generic smokes — something that Eddie in particular considered a disturbing trend.

"Meet The Hard Pack" was offered as a Camel Cash premium in the fourth Camel Cash Catalog. Thousands of them were ordered. And while it didn't go platinum, rumor has it that the recording sessions were so much fun, nobody cared.

"EMPTY LIGHTER BLUES"

I said it's early in the morning,
And that old clock's striking on two.
It's way over in the morning,
And that old clock's about to strike on two.
Just pulled out my Camel cigarettes,
But whoa, I just don't know what I'm gonna do.

I got the empty lighter blues.
I ain't got no butane.
I got the empty lighter blues,
I got no use for this thing.
Gonna get myself some striking matches
Before this lighter drives me insane.

I flicked it one times two,
Flicked it three times four,
I flicked that lighter 'til my thumb got sore.

I got the empty lighter blues.
I can't use this thing no more.
I'm gonna get myself some striking matches
Way on down at the corner store . . .

Max Matchbooks

One of four Hard Pack lighters offered during the Hard Pack's debut, this one featuring Max.

"Rooftop," 1992
This was the launch billboard for Camel 99's.

59

"Beach Chair," 1992

"WHEREVER JOE WENT, A PART OF EACH OF US WENT WITH HIM. WHEN HE WAS SITTING SIX FEET OFFSHORE IN A LOUNGE CHAIR, TICKLING HIS TOES IN THE WARM, TURQUOISE WATER, HE WAS JUST SITTING IN FOR US."

7

C L U B

CAMEL

"Hammock," 1991

"Sunrise at Club Camel," 1991

One of the things smokers purportedly liked best about Joe Camel was that he seemingly never worked. You never saw Joe wielding a greasy lug wrench or gossiping by the water cooler while he was waiting for the copy machine to get fixed. Joe's admirers admired him all the more because he was able to "get over," to transcend the less pleasant responsibilities of their own routine, workaday existences and truly enjoy the good life. (Something which the rest of us can only dream about—or sample in tiny, nouvelle-cuisine-sized portions if we're particularly fortunate.)

Joe was the King of Laid-Back. And one sandy corner of Joe's world that particularly epitomized his ability (and inclination) to kick back and chill out was Club Camel.

Situated on a small, private, dromedary-shaped island somewhere in the Caribbean, Club Camel had it all: beaches, nightlife, recreational activities galore,

"Island Tour," 1991

and a coterie of dedicated staff people who never gave "no" for an answer. It truly was a "Smooth Place to Be."

More than just a parody of Sunday-newspaper travel-section resort advertising, Club Camel represented instantly accessible escapism. Because wherever Joe went, a part of each of us went with him. When he was sitting six feet offshore in a lounge chair, tickling his toes in the warm, turquoise water, he was just sitting in for us. And when he was tickling the ivories for his friends at night with the Hard Pack backing him up, we could hear every Calypso beat just as clearly as if we were standing there under the tiki torches right along with them.

In short, when Joe said: "Wish You Were Here," it was with a knowing grin: he knew (as we knew) that it was an invitation we'd already been delighted to accept.

"Buried in the Sand," 1991

The Club Camel logo wound up on all kinds of things—including these cotton boxer shorts.

"Ordering Out," 1991

"Tropical Hard Pack," 1992

65

"Club Camel Coasterset," 1992

"Footprints," 1991

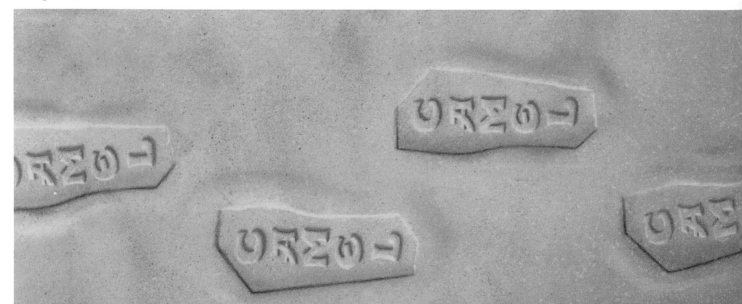

Matchbook with 5-day forecast

These Camel flip-flops left an impression of the Camel trademark typeface wherever you set foot in them.

VISIT
CLUB CAMEL
A SMOOTH PLACE TO BE

Club Camel Brochure, 1992

"New Year's '93," 1992

JOE AND THE OTHER CAMEL CHARACTERS

"

CELEBRATED JUST ABOUT EVERY HOLIDAY

THEY COULD FIND ON A

CALENDAR.

"

8

HAPPY
HOLIDAYS

"Thanksgiving at Max & Ray's," 1994

Octoberfest Point-of-Sale Piece, 1992

What would Octoberfest be without your own working stein? It'd be like Joe without his own custom lederhosen.

St. Patrick's Day Point-of-Sale piece, 1992

"Mardi Gras," 1991

was wasting vacation days. In the second place, none of 'em were married. So, no in-laws. And finally, they all got Camel Cash items for free — which made holiday shopping about as easy and convenient as it could be.

It's no wonder then that Joe and the other Camel characters celebrated just about every holiday they could find on a calendar. Whether it was a major one, the three-day-weekend kind, or just an obscure, regional day of observance, it was a good excuse to party. Not that Joe Camel ever really needed an excuse to do that.

"Bringing Home the Tree," 1994

"Mardi Gras II", 1993

"Celebrating Presidents' Day," 1992

In keeping with the spirit of the season, Joe and the gang would go caroling to the light of their butane lighters. On Thanksgiving, Max and his twin brother Ray would challenge each other to a duel with drumsticks. President's Day would find Joe and Max in presidential garb. And on Mardi Gras, Joe's favorite festival of them all, wherever he happened to be would transform magically into Bourbon Street and the holiday spirits would flow.

Joe and the Camel characters made sure that their holidays were always happy ones, and in a way they set an example for the rest of us to follow. But perhaps the best thing about the way they celebrated special occasions was something they didn't do: never, not once, did they have an After-Holiday Half-Off sale.

Holiday light sets come in all shapes, sizes, and colors. In the case of these Camel holiday lighters, they came five to a set.

"Handlebars." 1991

> "NEWER IS BETTER AND NEWEST IS BEST."

9

KEEPING THE CAMPAIGN MOVIN'

keeping the campaign movin'

"Pool Player," 1992

The marketplace is a fickle place. One day a recording artist can have three top-ten songs and a limo-ful of Grammys; the next day the same singer will be lucky to get booked on a late-late-night talk show behind a psychic sword-swallower, a trio of alien abductees, and the guy who invented the self-mowing lawn.

As consumers of pop culture, our appetite is voracious. If we've "been there and done that" before, chances are we won't give it a second look. Newer is better, and newest is best.

This behavioral principle is especially true when it comes to people selling us things. Heaven help the marketer that throws the same pitch for too long. By the time an ad campaign reaches the ripe old age of three (if it hasn't already been scrapped in favor of some new hare-brained idea du jour), finding ways to keep the idea fresh and unexpected becomes more and more of a challenge.

SURGEON GENERAL'S WARNING: Quitting Smoking Now Greatly Reduces Serious Risks to Your Health.

"Jukebox," 1991

"Golf," 1993

"Profile," 1991. Specially created for People Magazine's "50 Most Beautiful People" Issue, this ad capitalized on Joe's popularity and parodied the magazine's editorial at the same time..

"Mao Posters." They were simple, reverent and iconic in the way they portrayed Joe — just as artwork depicting the Chairman of the People's Republic of China was.

Greater attention was also paid at this time to the quality of the artwork as art. It was not unusual for an illustration to go back and forth between agency and artist five or six times — and then the retouching would start, another lengthy and painstaking process.

As a result, Joe's popularity didn't wane. If anything, the Big Guy got even bigger. A campaign that was unexpected to begin with had retained its unpredictable nature. And Camel had other surprises in store, too. Including one that could best be called an Election Year surprise.

personality, but references to Joe as "Smooth Character" have all but vanished. Instead the word "Camel" showed up in its own unique typeface. If you saw the finished ads in which the artwork shown here for "Pool Player" (p. 82) and "Golf" (p. 84) appeared, you would have seen that logo incorporated. The "bent" Camel logo provided a visual link back to the brand's classic pack iconography, and replaced the "Smooth Character" slogan in every case but one. And even that one "Hat Toss" (p. 86) supported the brand's Shake Things Up strategy, since it appeared more than a year after the last previous Smooth Character billboard had been posted. It was simply a fun "blast from the past."

Many of the pieces of Joe art from this era, including the one entitled "Handlebars" (p. 80) came to be known inside the ad agency as

"Pack Toss," 1995

"Brick Wall," 1993. This art was to appear on a brick wall in Chicago.

keeping the campaign movin'

"L.A. Standee," 1992

VOTE JOE

It was November, 1992. Incumbent George Bush was the Republican candidate for President. Former Arkansas Governor Bill Clinton was the Democratic nominee. Billionaire Ross Perot had nominated himself. But there was another party which sought to place a candidate on the ballot. The Camel Party.

Represented not by a donkey or an elephant but by a camel, the Camel Party billed itself as "The Party That Knows How to Party". And Joe, as you can imagine, was its candidate.

Over the course of the campaign, Joe's support grew and grew. People even sent in Camel Cash C-Notes just to help finance his run for office. It's not clear how many write-in votes Joe Camel received in the voting booths of America that year, but in the end it didn't really matter. He probably wouldn't have taken the job anyway.

Bumper stickers that went out to all Camel Party members.

Joe thanked his supporters with a personal thank-you note. If they'd contributed large amounts of Camel Cash, they got to visit his house and, you guessed it, spend the night in the "R.J. Bedroom."

Dear Camel Party Supporter,

The '92 election is right around the corner, and thanks to your support, my campaign is in full swing.

Ever since I declared my candidacy, things have really been smokin'. Smooth characters from across our great land have taken a stand against politics as usual and joined the Camel Party — The Party That Knows How to Party. Even if we don't get as many votes as the other guys, we'll definitely have better parties.

I just wanted to write and thank you personally for your generous support. Your C-Notes will go to good use as we take our message to the people. It's going to be a tough race, but with a little luck I'm sure that the best party will win.

Joe

P.S. Don't forget to vote. It's the smooth thing to do.

91

Joe accepting his party's nomination. Visual taken from a "Vote Joe" direct mail piece. Also shown: Some of the campaign buttons that helped propel Joe into national political prominence.

A *special issue of* Smooth Magazine *was planned, but only the cover was completed.*

Left: *"Wides Intro. Print Ad,"* 1992
Below: *Max & Ray, artwork from*
"Wides Teaser Billboard," 1992

Two of the more colorful characters in Joe's world were the ones who almost always dressed in nothing but black and white. Max, of Hard Pack fame, was joined by his twin brother Ray in 1992 for the introduction of Camel Wides—a wide-gauge cigarette that in many ways was (and still is) the ultimate Camel.

Wider (according to Max) and smoother (according to Ray) than any Camel cigarette before them, Camel Wides were the first new styles introduced and represented entirely by characters other than Joe. Wides' 1992 launch featured Max and Ray strutting their stuff (in this case, giant packs of the new product) on billboards, in print ads, and via direct mail pieces. Who better to endorse fat Camels than a couple of fat camels, right?

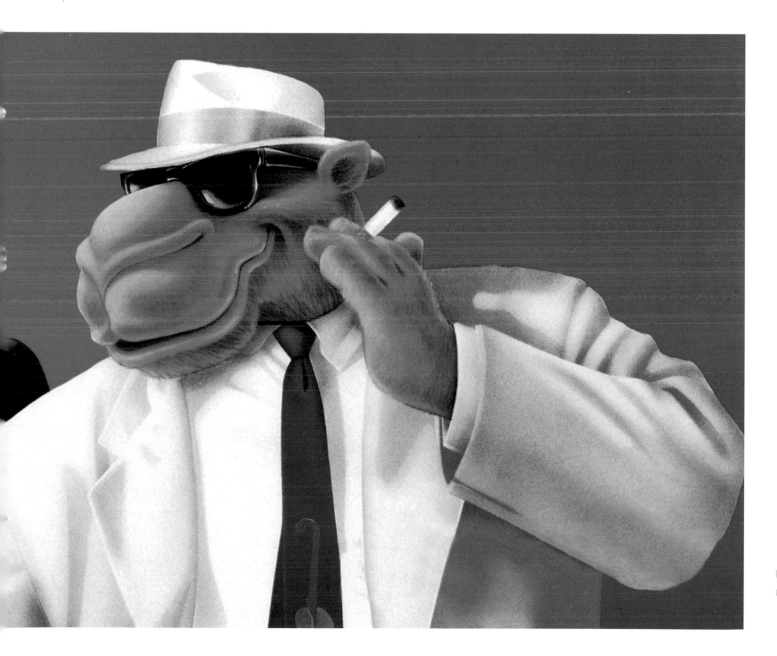

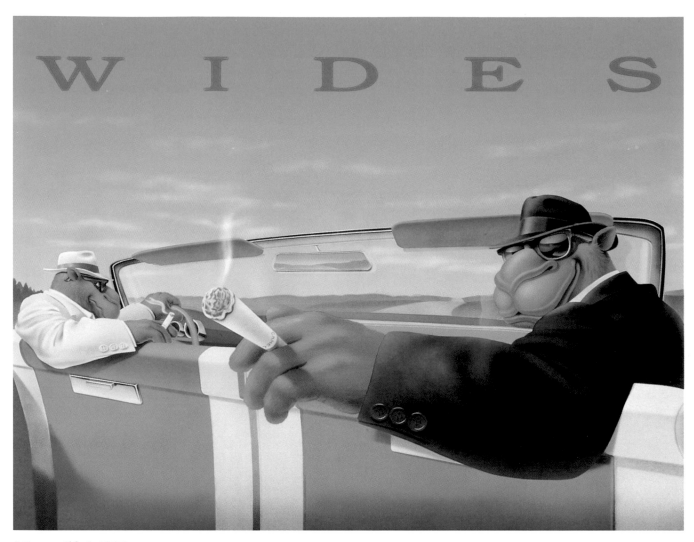

"Convertible," 1995

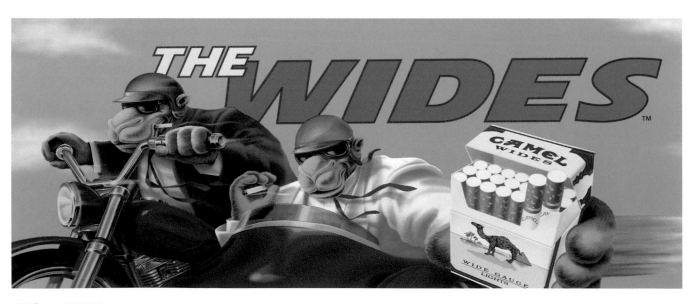

"Sidecar," 1992

"Couch Potato," 1996

But the brothers act didn't stop with the new product debut. Max and Ray, like so many archetypical twins before them, went on to contribute to the brand's image development in some rather unconventional ways. For if Joe was the Ambassador of Smooth, Max and Ray were more like something out of Vaudeville. They were offbeat, heretical, mischievous. And inseparable.

It may have been a "Wide, Wide World," but wherever Max went, Ray was his shadow. Or vice versa maybe. They did a lot of driving (on the wide open road, of course) often appearing in classic cars or their favorite two-man vehicle: a motorcycle with sidecar.

They also starred in their own radio program,

The Max & Ray Show. On the air, they debated important issues such as: "Why do we drive on parkways and park on driveways," and "How much dough would you be willing to lend to two strangers?" They also interviewed highly entertaining guests, like the Pizza Delivery Man. Which brings us to one other important thing you should know about Max and Ray.

They liked to eat. A lot. Thanksgiving Day at Max and Ray's was a two-turkey affair. On the air and off, they elevated talking with one's mouth full to an art form. And pity the poor family that tried to precede the Wides Guys to a buffet. The only thing worse would be following them to a buffet.

"Road Trip," 1992

Max & Ray two-sided ashtray, affectionately known as the "coming and going ashtray."

"Wides Postcard," 1992

"Wider & Smoother," 1992

"The Max & Ray Show," 1993. The Wides Guys weren't exactly shock-jocks, but they knew how to electrify an audience.

Camel Wides may not quite have taken the cigarette market by storm, but The Wides Guys themselves made a big impression when they appeared. Of course, they made big impressions whenever they sat down, too, but that's another story.

Max & Ray salt and pepper shakers: another way the Wides Guys showed up at the table.

The first Camel Cash magazine insert,
featuring Joe as George Washington, 1991

"CAMEL CASH . . . THE FUNNY
MONEY THAT'S NO
JOKE."

11

THE CURRENCY OF
THE REALM

Above and below: Camel Cash billboards, 1993

One of the peculiar things about living in today's modern American capitalistic society is that nobody pays full price for anything anymore. With discounts, sales, coupons, and buy-one-get-one-free offers, marketers in every category each try to out-promote the other in order to gain a greater market share for their wares. It's gotten to the point where deals are so prevalent that the expression, "What's The Deal?" has become a slang colloquialism synonymous with "What's Happening?"

Camel was one of the first cigarette brands to offer premium items to its adult smokers at retail. On any given week, with your purchase of two packs of Camels at your neighborhood convenience store, you could have gotten free playing cards, a free T-shirt, a free flashlight, a free keychain, a free hat, a couple of free lighters, or

EL CASH

The funny money that's no joke.

The four-page ad which introduced Camel Cash. It featured a pop-up Joe in the center offering magazine readers three free C-Notes. 1991.

dozens of other freebies. Not only did offers like these encourage adult smokers of other brands to try Camels, they helped dimensionalize Joe. You didn't just leave the store with a pack or two of smokes, you took a piece of Joe's World with you. Camel's imaginative promotions brought Joe Camel to life.

Ultimately, the program proved to be so popular that Camel decided to expand it. With Camel Cash, they were able to offer their much

sought-after merchandise week-in and week-out. With it, the brand could help bolster the loyalty of its smokers — and keep them from trading down to generic, low-priced smokes.

Camel Cash, "The Funny Money That's No Joke," changed the paradigm for promoting cigarette purchases. With one "C-Note" attached to each pack, and catalogs full of Camel merchandise to choose from, smokers no longer had to settle for whatever was offered in

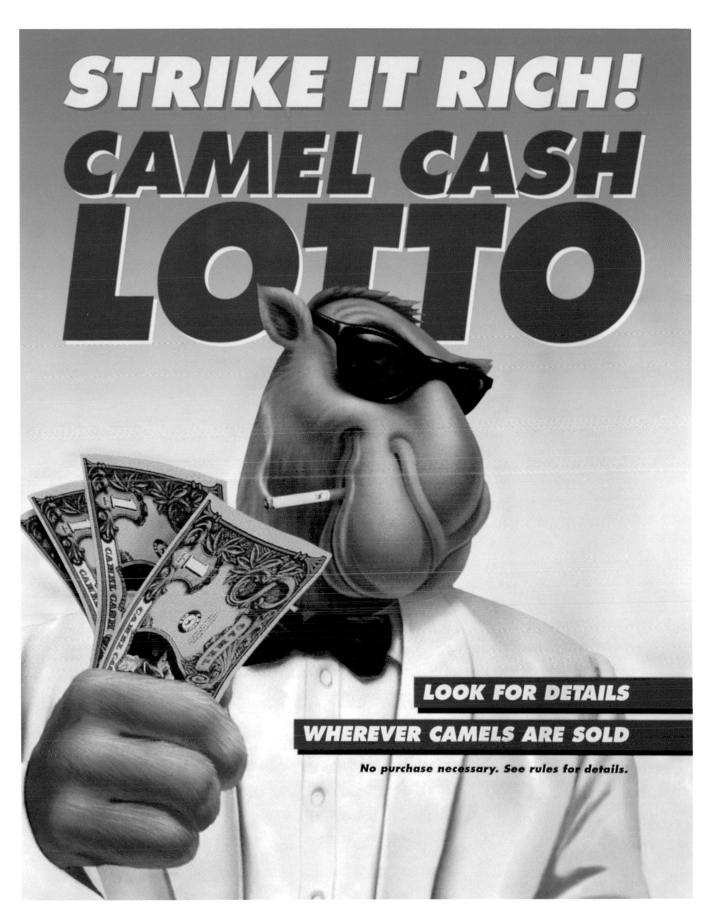

Magazine ad for Camel Cash Lotto, 1993.

the store. Instead, they could save up their C-Notes and "buy" whatever items they liked. From T-shirts to hats to beach towels to beer glasses, the Camel Cash catalogs offered a wide variety of merchandise. And millions of adult smokers saw it as an offer too good to refuse.

To date, there have been over a dozen editions of the Camel Cash catalog. Millions and millions of orders have been placed for merchandise. The program was so successful that Camel's biggest competitor, Marlboro, followed Camel's lead and offered its smokers catalogs of merchandise as well.

Camel Cash merchandise has always been in high demand. Countless letters have been written to Camel (many addressed to Joe) in which people begged for this or that out-of-stock item. One woman even wrote to say that her boyfriend had left her, taking all of her C-Notes — and her Hard Pack Shower Curtain! She didn't care about the boyfriend, or the C-Notes; she could find more of both. But the shower curtain was no longer being offered and she couldn't bear the idea of showering without it.

Secondary markets sprung up — for both Camel Cash premiums and for Camel Cash itself. Bartenders would routinely search the bars at night's end to find any discarded C-Notes to add to their treasure chests. It wasn't unusual for Camel to receive orders for merchandise totaling a thousand C-Notes or more from smokers who'd been saving up for years.

Many of the catalogs themselves were themed. One that was particularly well received was the Camel Cash Lotto Catalog. In that catalog, not only could you order items like a Joe "Pop Art" T-shirt, you could enter a drawing for a chance to win a million C-Notes. Which you could then spend on things like a 1963 Corvette, or Joe's Harley-Davidson Fat Boy motorcycle, or a Jeep Wrangler painted in a custom Camel paint-job. Needless to say, it was one of the most popular catalogs Camel ever produced.

Camel Cash merchandise ranged from the utilitarian to the bizarre. In fact, the book you're reading was offered in the Camel Cash Timeless Collectibles Catalog. Will it appreciate in value as much as some of the other Camel merchandise has? Only time will tell. But this much is certain: the Camel Cash program brought Joe's world to life in our world. And led to the kind of brand loyalty that only funny money can buy.

Camel has produced more than a dozen Camel Cash catalogs. Some are shown here, along with a sampling of favorite items offered.

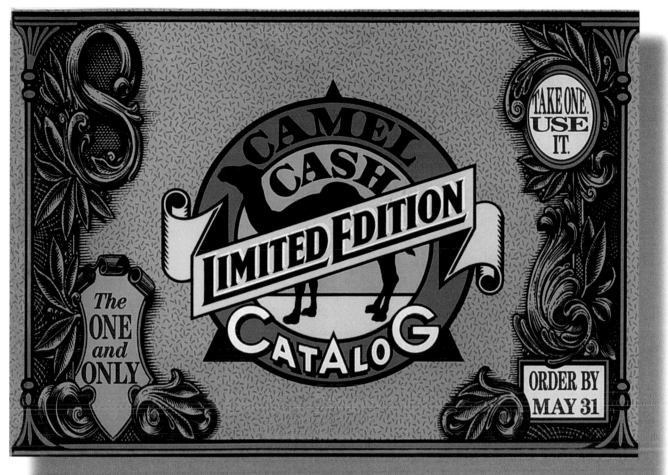

Catalog #1, 1991

Hard Pack shower curtain, Catalog #1

Joe's Head can hugger, Catalog #1

CAMEL.

The Official
Camel Cash Catalog
VOLUME IV

Joe Camel Sightings Reported!

Camel's 80th Anniversary.

Special Offer for Special Lights Smokers!

Catalog #4, 1993

*Camel Custom Jeep Wrangler, offered as
a sweepstakes prize, Catalog #4*

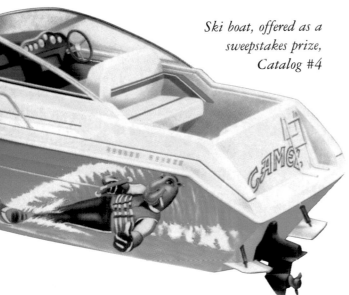

Ski boat, offered as a sweepstakes prize, Catalog #4

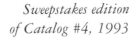

Sweepstakes edition of Catalog #4, 1993

Hard Pack poker set, Catalog #5

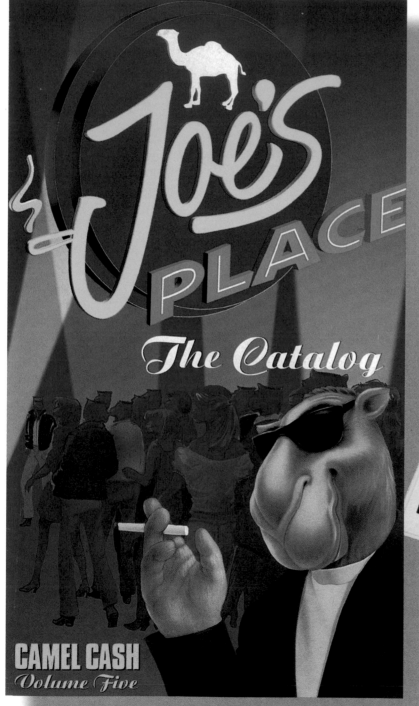

Catalog #5, 1994

Joe Pop Art beach towel,
Catalog #5

Joe's Tank Top, Catalog #6

Catalog #6, 1995

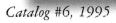

Pool Player playing cards and rack-shaped tin, Catalog #6

Hard Goods Catalog, 1995

Road Trip Catalog, 1996

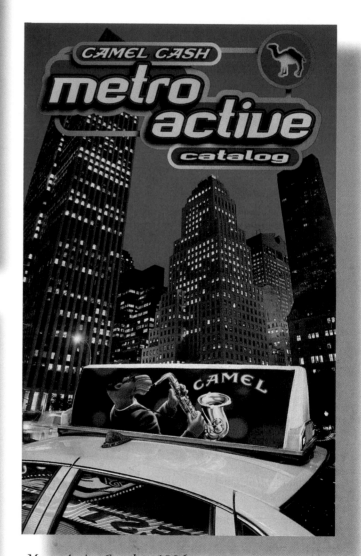

Metro-Active Catalog, 1996

Timeless Collectibles Catalog, 1997

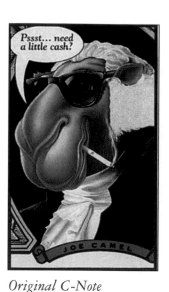

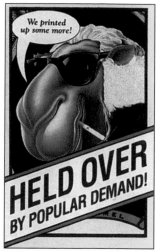

Here's how the C-Notes appeared on packs:

Original C-Note

2nd C-Note

3rd C-Note

Here is the inside of the C-Note covers shown above.

THE ALMIGHTY C-NOTE

As Camel Cash Catalog number two proclaimed: "Your Money's No Good Here!" Only Camel Cash C-Notes could be exchanged for merchandise. And the C-Note itself has quite a story to tell. Originally part of a short-term, limited-time promotion, Camel Cash C-Notes were held over, doubled, redesigned countless times, and offered in an ever-growing range of denominations over the course of the program.

To date, Camel has printed and distributed *billions* of Camel Cash C-Notes on packs of Camels. That's billions, with a B. Enough C-Notes that

Single panel C-Note (still with Joe as George).

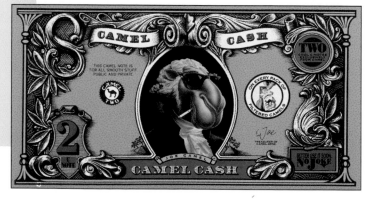

The Camel Cash 2-Spot. It originally appeared on packs of Camel Special Lights.

The Camel Cash 3-Spot. It saw very limited circulation and is the rarest of all C-Notes.

Two different 5-Spots were designed, each featuring Max.

if you laid them end to end, they'd circle the Earth at the equator many times over. Enough that if you stacked them up you'd have a pile several times as tall as Mt. Everest.

Shown here are some of the design changes made to the 1-Note, as well as several C-Notes of higher denominations which saw limited distribution, mostly in conjunction with special offers.

Can anybody change a twenty?

The Camel Cash 10-Spot. You had to be a high roller to get your hands on these.

The ultimate in Camel Cash: The 50 C-Note Certificate.

THE DRAWING BOARD

With dozens of new items needed every year for appearance in Camel Cash Catalogs, the pressure was always on to find unique premiums to offer. Sometimes, though, as you'll see by looking at some of these ideas, the pressure was too much. Gotta give 'em credit for trying, though.

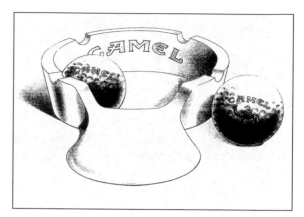

Camel Putting Cup/Ashtray

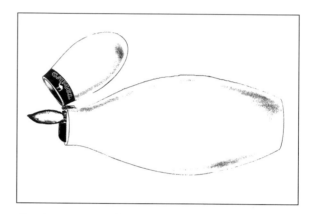

Bowling Pin Lighter

Hunting Cap

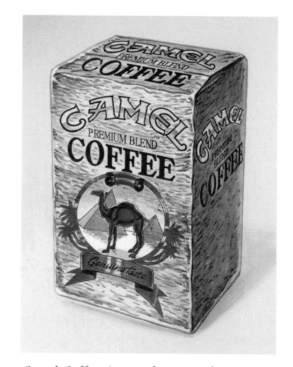

Camel Coffee. Anyone for a cup of Joe?

Bar-B-Q Mitt

Hard Pack Wind Chimes

Hard Pack "Fan Hat"—an idea that really blew.

Pool Player "Elbow" Mug. This item is the only Camel Cash item which actually did make it into a catalog but then was never produced. When all was said and done, the supplier couldn't figure out how to make it. Those who ordered one got a refund, some bonus C-Notes and an apology—but no mug.

Bridge. 1993

"CAMEL SPECIAL LIGHTS WAS AN ENTIRELY DIFFERENT PRODUCT. ITS ADVERTISING WAS DIFFERENT, TOO."

12

A LIGHT TO
REMEMBER

Taste Camel in a Whole New Light

a light to remember

"Balcony," 1993

There's an old saying: You can please all of the people some of the time, and you can please some of the people all of the time, but you can't please all the people all the time. It's a true saying as far as it goes, but what the people at Camel would hasten to add is that it never hurts to try.

The addition of Special Lights to the Camel product lineup was an attempt to do just that.

It happened in 1993, five years after Joe hit the scene. Camel Lights were extremely popular. But there were still a lot of smokers who preferred the even-lighter, white-tipped Marlboro Lights product. So, after a lot of internal debate about breaking with tradition, Camel decided to add a smoother, white-tipped product to its lineup. And Camel Special Lights was born.

Camel Special Lights was an entirely different product. Its advertising was different, too.

The Special Lights campaign revolved around the idea of romance. Joe was shown on a beach, in the moonlight, holding a rose or sitting on a beach chair. The sky was the coolest of blues and Joe was nattily attired in a white sport coat. The colors and theme of the advertising were meant to reflect the mildness of the new product, while the rose in his hand or lapel was a signal that, for this product launch at least, Joe had settled down. He had become a kinder, gentler Joe.

In the Special Lights ads, Joe took a break from the frenzied, party lifestyle of his earlier years. A "significant other" was even hinted at — and shown from behind in one ad. But she was never showcased. It was still Joe's show.

By the time 1993 had run its course, though, Joe had tired of this more subdued lifestyle and had decided to return to more active pursuits. The Joe who'd graced the Special Lights advertising would be seen no more. The white jacket would be relegated to the back of his walk-in closet. And Joe would move on to bigger, if not better, things.

The Camel Special Lights Diamond Ashtray—one of the best-sellers from the fourth Camel Cash Catalog, 1993.

"Moonlight," 1993

"Beach Chairs," 1993

"Moonlight Spread," 1993

"T.J.," 1993

"EARLY ATTEMPTS AT RENDERING
AN ACCEPTABLE FEMALE CAMEL
MET WITH DISASTER."

13

AN IDEA WHOSE TIME HADN'T COME

female camel met with disaster. The camel women either wound up looking too much like camels or they wound up looking like some other kind of animal (notably, sheep—or even worse, dogs).

After months of development, though, a suitable female camel was created. And after days of discussion about how she should be dressed, and what kind of name would position her as both feminine and "nobody's fool," she was christened "T.J."

But that was far from the end of it. Because now that the Camel marketing group and its agency had proven they *could* portray a

female equivalent to Joe, the question arose: *should* they?

Many smokers liked T.J. Others were not so keen on her. But in the end, adding a love interest to Joe's supporting cast of characters was seen as too distracting. So after months of exploration, brainstorming, and research, the idea of having a female friend for Joe was canned.

With the grand opening of Joe's Place in 1994, female camels would eventually get their day in the sun. But the concept of giving Joe a steady girlfriend never flew. He just wasn't the kind of guy that anyone wanted to see get tied down.

"Cruise Ship," 1993

"Motorcycle" (2 versions), 1993. These two illustrations demonstrate just how polarizing the introduction of a female camel was. Men wanted Joe to be in charge at all times; he'd never ride on the back of a motorcycle. But women wanted T.J. to assert herself, too. They preferred her to be driving. The twain could not meet.

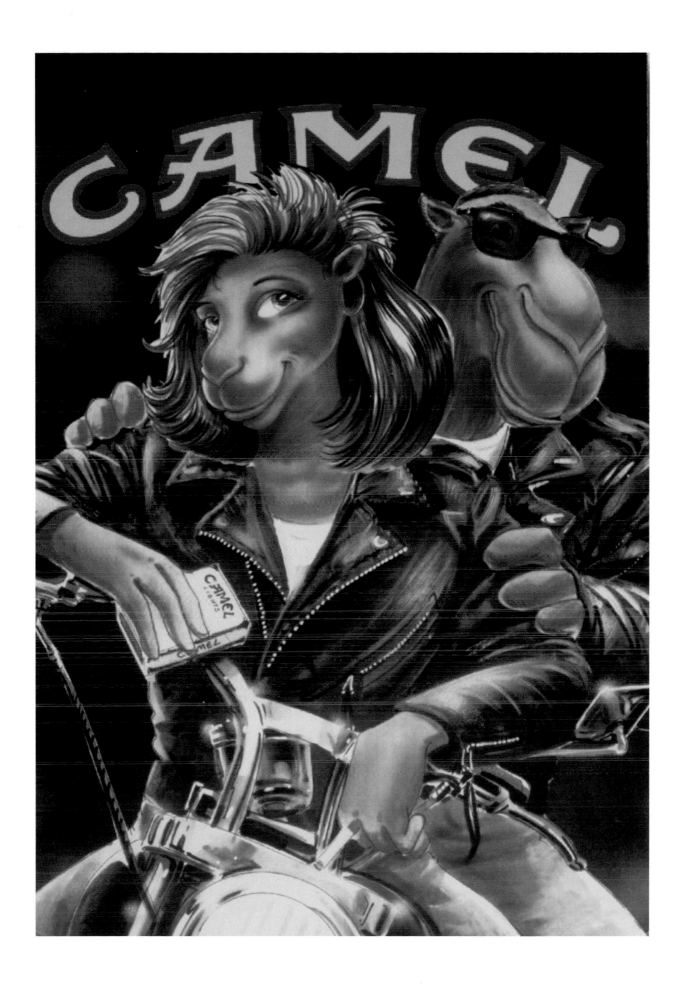

"Flowers," 1992. *Joe always had a romantic side, but would he ever have a girlfriend?*

"Softball," 1993

"The Grand Opening of Joe's Place," 1994

JOE'S PLACE

There may not have been room for female camels at Joe's side, but there was certainly room for them in his club. In fact, there was room for just about everything at Joe's Place. You could shoot pool there, dance to the music of The Hard Pack, pick up a Joe's Place T-shirt, or just hang out with other camel guys—or camel women. Oh, and you could smoke there, too.

Joe's Place was "Midnight at The Oasis" times three. Camels of every kind congregated there. But it was the appearance of camel women that differentiated the Joe's Place advertising from Camel ads that preceded it. It was the first time that the faces of female camels, as opposed to those of human women, appeared in Camel advertising.

The idea, of course, depended on the female camels being there. A huge bar room filled with nothing but camel guys, after all, would have sent quite a different message.

It was expected that the debut of the female Camels would generate a good deal of surprise in the marketplace. And there was a good deal of talk, but not about the female camels. In fact, the Joe's Place campaign proved to be very popular among adult smokers. They weren't surprised, however. It was almost as if female camels had been a part of Joe's world all along. It seemed natural for them to be there, just as it seemed natural for Joe to have a night club all his own.

As the copy in the ads stated, Joe's place offered "something for everyone." But maintaining the quality of the artwork at such a grand scale proved to be a formidable task. Fortunately, though, Joe's Place was but one station stop for a campaign that never stopped anywhere for long. The campaign soon shifted back to portraying Joe in more iconic ways. And after a lot of long nights at Joe's Place, agency art directors were finally able to get some sleep.

Joe made sure everyone visiting his place had two things—a good time, and their own ashtray.

Joe's Place, Smokin', 1994

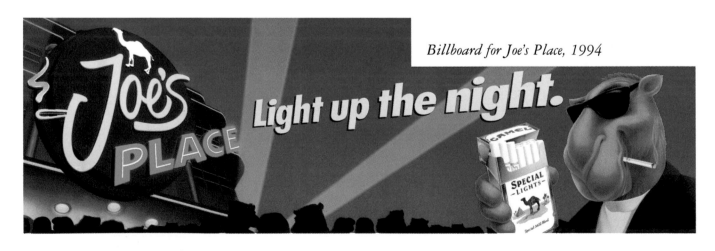

Billboard for Joe's Place, 1994

The art for this Joe's Place magazine ad, 1994, was actually made up of several separate scenes which were retouched together to create one big bar room full of camels. Producing the art in that way was a lot of work, but it enabled Camel to shift things around and depict the goings-on at Joe's in ads of many different shapes and sizes.

"Riding into Town," 1995

"CAMEL HAS BEEN A FAVORITE
OF MOTOCYCLE ENTHUSIASTS FOR AS
LONG AS THEY'VE BEEN STRAPPING
ON THEIR LEATHERS."

14

RIDING WITH THE
PACK

The Camel Roadhouse on the main drag in Daytona during Bike Week, '95.

"Armpit," 1996

Daytona Beach, Florida and Laconia, New Hampshire, to name but a few.

At each event, The Camel Roadhouse gives bikers a place to hear music, grab a cold beverage, compare tattoos, even get their boots shined. It's the party to end all parties. And it's Camel's way of thanking bikers for the loyalty they've shown to the brand over the years.

If you've never been to Sturgis or one of the other rally sites during Bike Week, zip into your gear and go check it out. And if you spot a white bike with a pyramid and palm trees on the tank, you'll know you've come to the right place.

Genuine Taste/Biker logo matchbook

A Camel premium designed expressly for Bike Week.

Joe's custom ride.

"Looking Down," 1996

"IF YOU'RE GOING TO INTRODUCE A MENTHOL STYLE, THE ADS HAVE GOT TO BE GREEN."

15

A CAMEL OF A DIFFERENT COLOR

"Harborview," 1997

"Tailfin," 1996

There's a rule in cigarette advertising: if you're going to introduce a menthol style, the ads have got to be green. Otherwise, even the most prominent typographic message will be ignored entirely and the ad will be seen as just another cigarette ad. Without that color cue, the word "MENTHOL" might as well be written in hieroglyphics. But with it, the word stands out like a neon sign. Go figure.

Color was a crucial element of the Camel campaign from the word Joe. The vibrant primary colors of the "Smooth Character" era, the purples and yellows of later ads and of Camel's point-of-sale signage, the bronze fur tones of the characters themselves—together they reflected a bold, modern palette that was hard to ignore and easy to recognize.

When focus groups were asked why they liked the Joe Camel ads, invariably one of the answers given was that it was because of "the colors." Of course, to hang their appeal on color alone would be an oversimplification. But there's no doubt that it played a central role in building Camel's image as a fun, imaginative brand.

"Polishing," 1996

In these Camel Menthol ads, most of which appeared in 1996, the key color is, of course, green. Had to be. Even the sky was green. But the colors which were used to play off against that green are pure Camel. There's the purply-pink of Joe's vintage car. The deep blue of Bustah's vest. The rich brown of his guitar. And the bright reds of the characters' jackets. Unlike most other brands, which attempt to carve their identities out of a single color and then do everything they can to "own" that color, Camel seemed to own *all* colors—indeed to own color itself.

It was, and still is, a successful strategy for Camel. And it only makes sense, since Joe and his buddies were some pretty colorful characters, too.

"Brooklyn Bridge," 1996

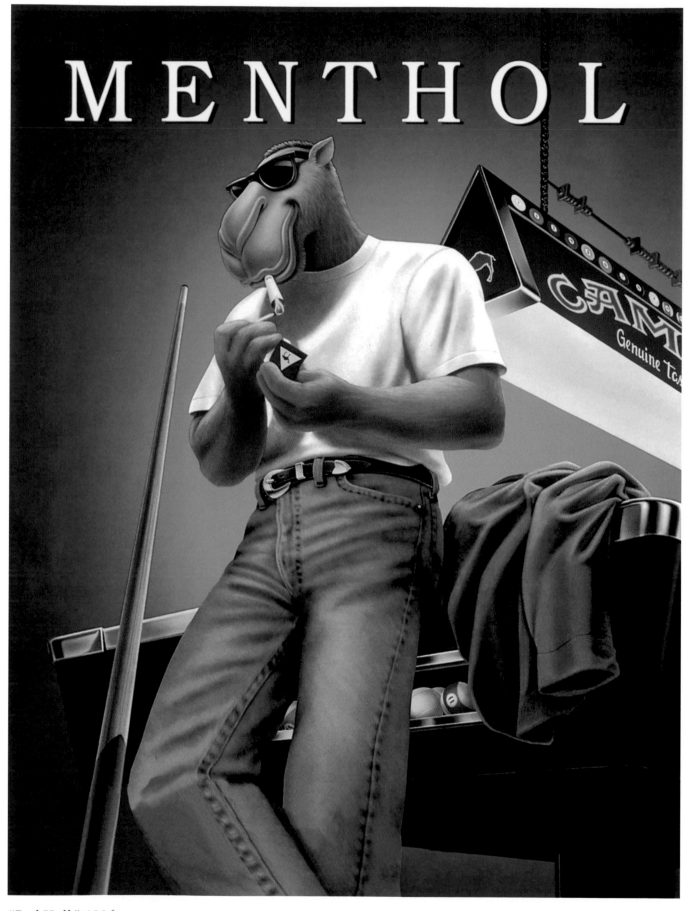

a camel of a different color

"Pool Hall," 1996

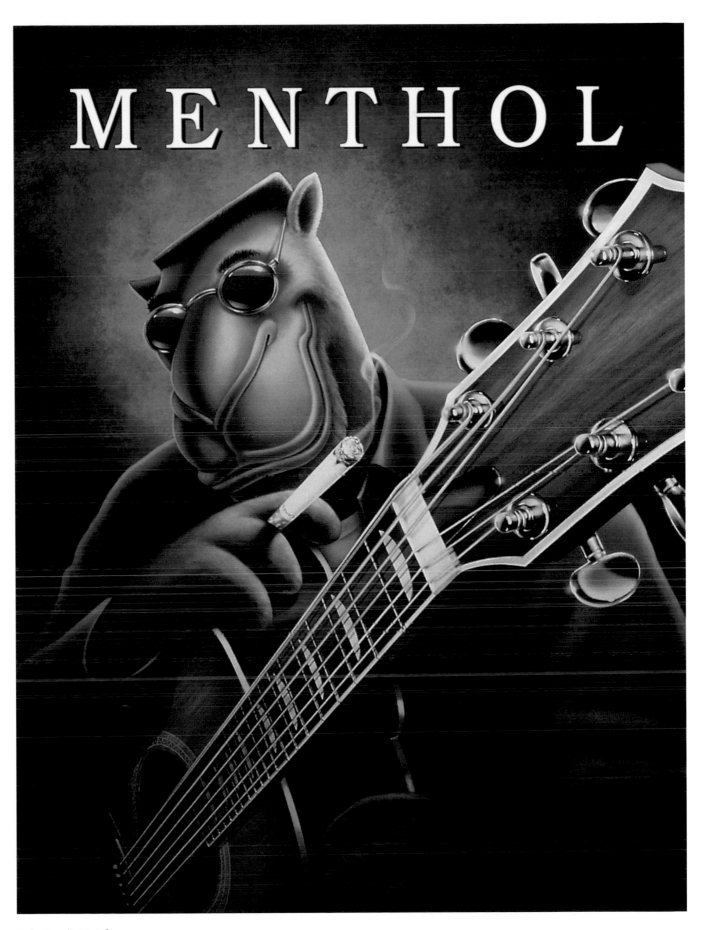

"Guitar," 1996

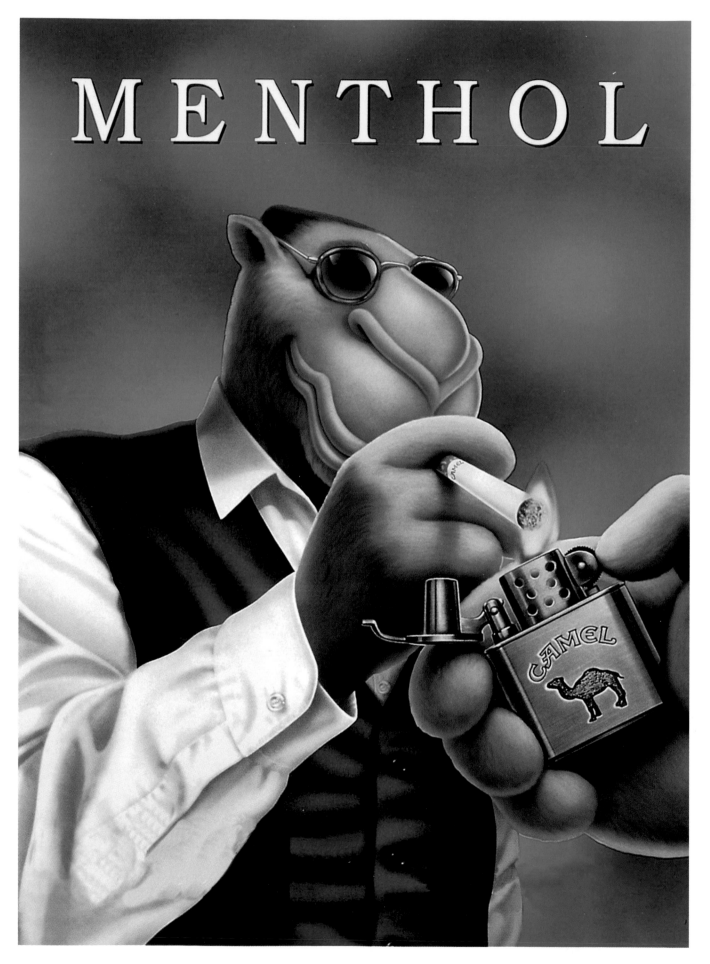

"Lighting," 1996

"Park Bench," 1997

"Top Down," 1996

"Sax Solo," 1997

"Convertible Pack," 1996

"WHEN JOE GOT BEHIND THE WHEEL,

IT WAS ALMOST AS IF HE WERE

ESCAPING THE RAT RACE

FOR ALL OF US."

16

TRAVELS WITH
JOE

"Hood Up," 1995

M uscle cars. Pickups. Motorcycles. Convertibles. If it's got wheels and it moves, somebody in America wants to gas it up and go. We are a nation with ants in its pants. Everybody's got places to go, people to see — and heaven help the poor schmuck who gets in our way.

Ever since the first wagon trains rolled west, getting out of Dodge and hitting the road has been one of America's favorite pastimes. The freedom of the open highway, the anticipation of adventures yet to be lived, the sinfully greasy food served up at every roadside diner — these are the things that four-wheeled fantasies are made of.

When Joe got behind the wheel, which he did fairly frequently, it was almost as if he were escaping the rat race for all of us. Whatever he was driving, wherever he was going, we were along for the ride. It didn't matter that we were on our way to work a double-shift when we spotted Joe riding his motorcycle on that 48-foot-wide billboard. For a second or two it was easy to imagine that we were riding with his pack — and leaving the nine-to-five routine in the dust.

"Stick Shift," 1996

"Red Motorcycle," 1996

It isn't surprising that Joe and the other Camel characters were so often depicted going mobile. Vehicles say things about their owners, and in Joe's case one of the things they said was that Joe had a large garage. But beyond that, there's a definite level of status associated with gleaming new motorcycles and cherry restorations. Everybody may want them, but only a select few will make the commitment to owning one. For Joe, a confirmed bachelor and adventurer, it was a commitment that was easy to make. He never stayed in one place for long. And with such an impressive selection of vehicles to choose from, there was no reason why he should have. When Joe rode off into the sunset in 1997, you can be sure he was riding in style.

From an art standpoint, this group of illustrations continued the design evolution which began with the Camel Menthol introduction. Rather than depicting the characters in a standard "snapshot" format, exaggerated angles and perspectives were used to heighten the impact of the imagery. Ads like"Hood Up," "Stickshift," and "Red Motorcycle" made the most of the magic of illustration and showed that not only were Joe and his pals going places, the campaign's artwork was, too.

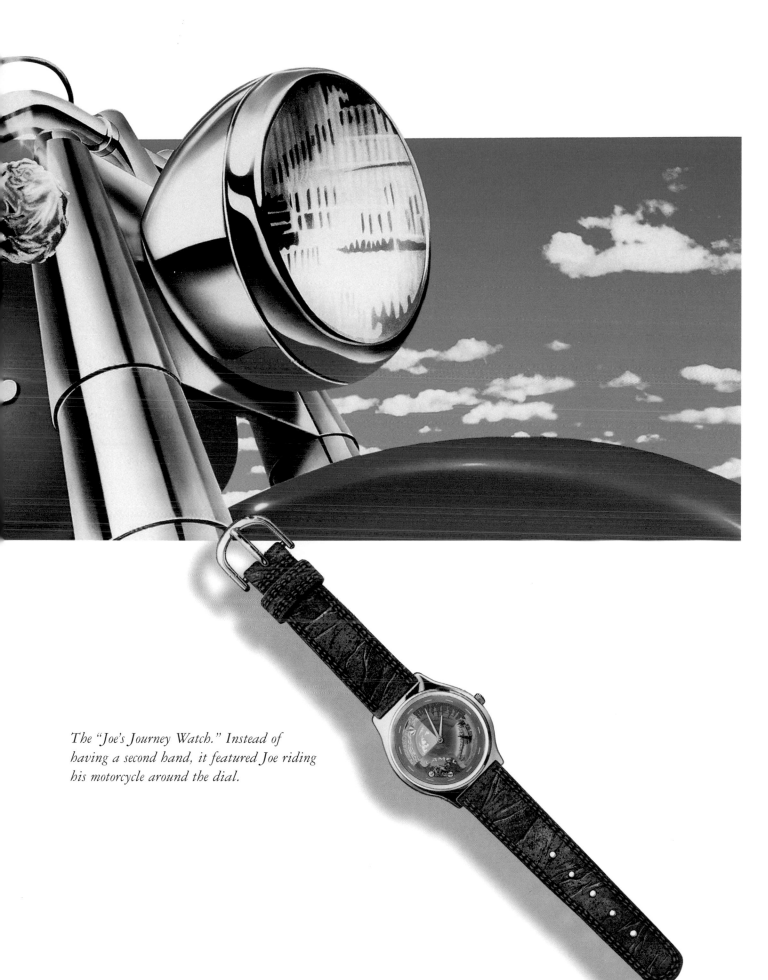

The "Joe's Journey Watch." Instead of having a second hand, it featured Joe riding his motorcycle around the dial.

"Roadhouse," 1996

"Rear View," 1996

"Never Boring," 1995

NEVER SAY NEVER

Despite all the times they'd resisted the temptation, despite all the arguments about not sinking to that level, despite all the marketing rules that command you to stick to your own game plan, this was one time that the people at Camel just couldn't resist poking fun at the good ole cowboy.

Part of an effort to reinforce Camel's heritage, its authenticity, and its "genuine" taste profile, this ad was a one-shot dig at all things Marlboro. Although meant in fun, there was also an element of competitive mudslinging to the concept. What could be more insulting, after all, than being called boring?

"Roulette Wheel," 1996

CAMEL

"NEW YORK MAY BE THE CITY
THAT DOESN'T SLEEP, BUT VEGAS
IS THE TOWN THAT DOESN'T
EVEN NAP."

17

VIVA LAS
VEGAS

viva las vegas

"Security Camera," 1996

If there's one place Joe Camel belonged, if there's one city that he should have had all the keys to, it's without a doubt Las Vegas. New York may be the City That Doesn't Sleep, but Vegas is the Town That Doesn't Even Nap. Twenty-four hours a day, people from all walks of life pay their money and take their chances at becoming rich, rich, rich beyond their wildest dreams. It's the most optimistic place on earth. So it's no surprise that Joe and his Hard Pack pals spent the better part of 1996 walking the strip and raking in the chips.

Joe was nothing if not optimistic. He didn't sit down at the craps table, or the blackjack table, or the high-stakes poker table expecting to lose his shirt. Joe was a winner. Whether he was shooting pool and clearing the table in one turn, playing golf and scoring in the mid-20's (for 18 holes), or letting his sizable winnings ride at the roulette wheel, Joe came out on top. Things just went his way. And that was one of the reasons he was so well-liked.

"Chip Flip," 1996
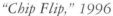

"Card Toss," 1996

Unlike other personalities, whose good fortune often tends to be viewed with resentment and jealousy, Joe was never begrudged his success. Maybe it's because he was just an illustrated character, or maybe it's because he was seen as the underdog in his battle to keep his "job" as Camel's spokesguy. Either way, we just hoped that Joe, against all odds, would continue to find a way to come out on top.

And Joe, being Joe, wasn't about to let us down.

"Dice," 1996

"Shades," 1996

The Roulette Wheel ashtray.

From there you went on to the virtual reality room and played some head games. You even went for the ride of your life on a Smokin' Joe's Racing simulator.

By then you were hungry. And thirsty. So you sashayed over to the Oasis and grabbed a cold one and a bite to eat under a neon palm tree. You sat on the biggest pillow you'd ever seen. And you weren't alone.

Satiated, you decided to saunter over to the Turkish Bazaar and find something to do with all the free C-Notes you'd been given. In the tents and cabanas of the Bazaar, you were amazed by the skills of a legion of belly dancers, snake charmers, sword swallowers, and contortionists. You were also amazed by your good fortune, as you parlayed your little pile of C-Notes into a much bigger one at the craps, roulette, and blackjack tables. Of course, you quit while you were ahead and knowing a great souvenir when you saw one, spent your winnings on elite Camel Cash merchandise.

Later on, after you had a chance to kick back and watch a live camel do some laps around the room, you caught a professional pool player demonstrating some trick shots. And before the night was over, you joined a thousand swaying bodies as Big Head Todd and the Monsters, The Smithereens, and Southern Culture on the Skids rocked the palace with their own special brands of alternative sound.

It was the kind of party that only Joe could have dreamed up.

Your basic Lampa las Lava, done Camel-style.

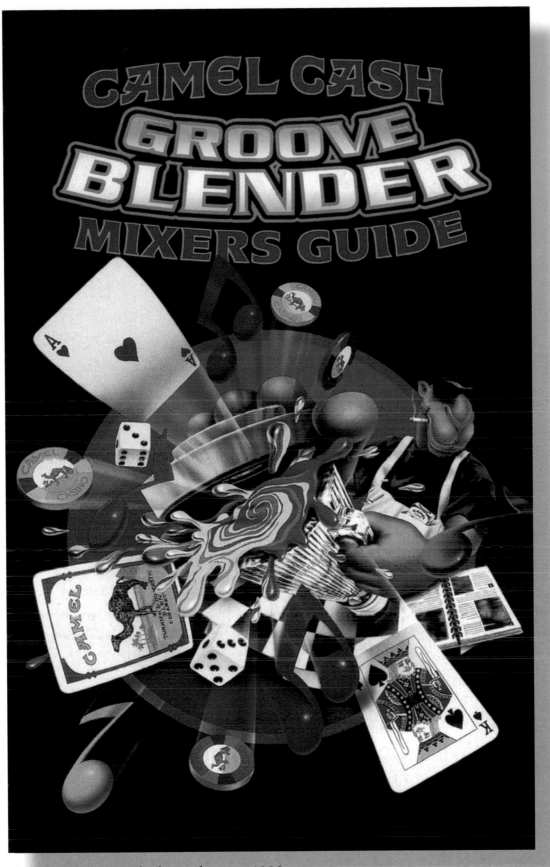

Camel Cash Groove Blender catalog cover, 1996

"Downpour," 1997

"UNFORGETTABLE. . .
THAT'S WHAT HE
WAS. "

18

ONE IN A
MILLION

"Joe City," 1997

From humble beginnings in the mind of some marketer, Joe Camel rose to dizzying heights of advertising success. His reign as spokescamel for his cigarette brand of choice spanned nine years in all. He appeared more often on network television newscasts than the Supreme Court Justices — who for many reasons never got to hear him plead his case. People loved him and people hated him. (One couple actually sent Joe a wedding invitation; due to scheduling conflicts, he couldn't go — though he did send a present.) But whichever side of the fence you were on, you knew who he was. Joe stood out in real life — in our world — just as he does in that sea of umbrellas. Unforgettable . . . that's what he was.

Do an Internet search for references to Joe Camel today and you'll still find over 400,000 listings — none of which were encouraged or authorized by R.J. Reynolds. Even though the campaign is gone now, you can still find news reports about Joe, editorial pieces, satiric parodies of Camel ads, political cartoons, and sundry other items.

"Diner," 1996

The Joe Camel campaign touched on countless aspects of popular American culture over the course of the years that it ran. Movies, music, politics, sports. Nightlife, money, urban living, history. Philosophy, fashion, travel, and even food. Joe's world was a complete world, and in the last year the campaign ran there was no need to add to it.

The ads in this chapter are the penultimate ones in the Joe Camel campaign. And, as you can see by looking at them, there was no attempt made to recreate the wheel. Classic themes of sociability, recreation, and entertainment still dominated. The artwork itself may be more sophisticated, more "photographic" in a sense, but that was simply a function of evolution — and of practicing making perfect. After nine years, the people who made

these ads knew what worked. And they knew what they liked, too.

One of the things they liked was that despite Joe's larger-than-life persona, he was at heart a very down to earth kind of guy. These final ads respect and reflect that. They show him hanging out with his buddies on a fire escape. Having a

The Joe's Diner clock was one good way to be on time for dinner. The other was never to leave Joe's Diner.

"Darts," 1996

"Fire Escape," 1997

cup of coffee in a diner. Throwing a game of darts. And bowling. What could be more commonplace than bowling?

If one ad in particular epitomizes the way his creators looked at Joe toward the end, it would have to be "Crosswalk" (see page 196). In that ad, Joe is crossing a quiet city street, alone. But

the angle at which Joe is shown, almost as if we are looking up at him with respect, is a good reflection of the esteem in which Joe was held to the very end.

He may have been on his way out, but this was, after all, still Joe. And with us or without us, he was still going places.

"Coffee Shop," 1997

one in a million

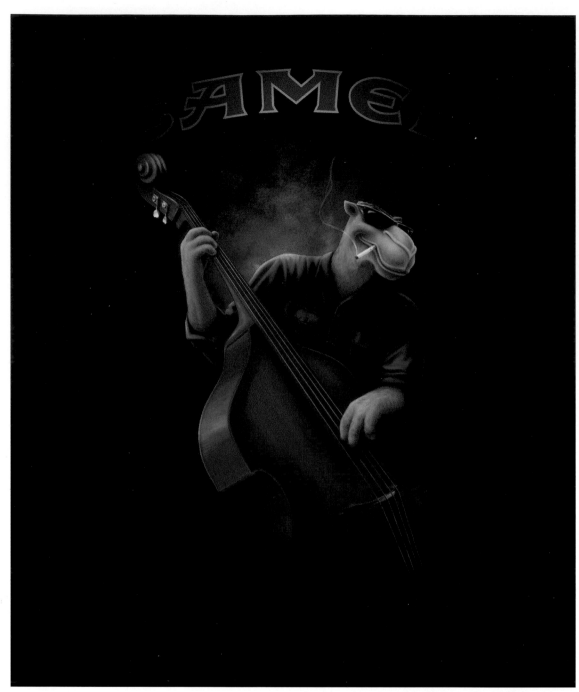

"Bass," 1996

"Throwing Darts," 1996

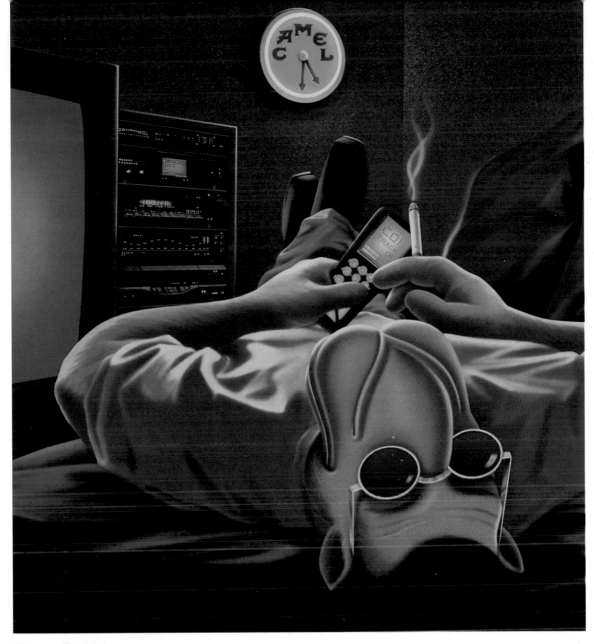

"Remote," 1997

"Bowling," 1997

FINAL NOTES

It happened the way Joe would have preferred: with no fanfare, no gnashing of teeth, no changing-of-the-guard ceremony. After nine years of appearing on billboards and in print ads, in direct mail pieces and on point-of-sale pieces, Joe simply vanished. He didn't even say goodbye.

In the days and weeks following Joe's retirement, a lot was written in the press about him. And in retrospect, it seems more than a little ironic that a simple advertising character, a two-dimensional figment of someone's imagination who was in reality nothing more than paint on paper, garnered so much attention. Joe may have been a vibrant departure from run-of-the-mill advertising, but he was, after all, just a smoking camel. A visual pun, plain and simple.

Or was he something more than that?

Joe Camel left his fans and his cigarette brand a great legacy. To his fans, Joe was more than just a clever advertising character. He was a friend. For the Camel brand, Joe was the guru who put a new face on a classic, old trademark.

All the imagination that went into the creation of almost ten years of advertising didn't go out the window when Joe exited stage-left. The colorful irreverence that Joe had personified ever since 1988 still lives on in our memories — and in this book.

Any way you look at him, Joe Camel was one of a kind. And even though he stayed around for less than a decade, he made his mark in ways that few advertising characters ever have or ever will. Joe's style, his attitude, his *joie de vivre*, made his mythological world seem magical. And it made our world seem a bit more magical, too.

He will be missed.

"Taps," 1997. The last ad to run in the Joe campaign featured not Joe, but Max playing one final tune before they called last call.

Finished artwork for "Crosswalk," 1997

The initial marker "Comp."

One of the more unusual letters Camel's ad agency received over the years was one from someone in Georgia who wrote to ask how the Joe Camel ads were shot. What that someone evidently didn't know was that Joe was much too busy to pose for a photograph every time the agency wanted to feature him in an ad. His schedule would never have allowed it. What's more, it probably would've been too expensive, what with location scouting, wardrobe, travel, photographer's fees, film processing costs, etc., etc.

No, the Joe ads were illustrated. By a small number of nationally recognized illustrators who had shown a proven knack for getting Joe's image right. But as talented as those artists were, no ad came easy. It was a long, involved process that usually took months of give and take, back and forth, faxing and fax-back-ing. The artwork shown with this section will give you some idea of what was involved.

Starting with an idea, a basic concept, the agency's art director gets a "comp" drawn (see "A"). Usually, it's just a marker drawing that's simply meant to represent the rough idea. Once everyone who matters says the idea's okay, it's sent out to an illustrator to begin the process of creating final artwork.

The illustrator's first step is to provide a series of pencil sketches (see "B"). Then the back and forth begins. Between sketch "B" and sketch "H", a dialogue takes place, with artist and art director focusing on creating just the right body language, perspective, and overall appearance for Joe himself. The comments written on every other sketch are those of the art director.

Once the pencil drawing of Joe looks right, the illustrator begins the process of placing Joe in the given environment — in this case, a city street. The next three sketches ("I," "J," and "K") show this process evolving. Finally, the complete pencil sketch is finished to everyone's satisfaction ("L"). Now the process of painting can begin.

It takes anywhere from two weeks to a month for the artist to complete the painting process. Getting the right mood, finding the right mix of colors, and rendering the characters' faces and "fur" tones are not something that can just be dashed off in a night or two of frenzied inspiration.

And there are bound to be changes along the way. In the case of this ad, R.J. Reynolds' legal staff noticed at the last minute that there were no crosswalk stripes

"H"—*final character pencil sketch;* "I"—*first pencil sketch of character in environment;* "J"—*second pencil sketch of character in environment;* "K"—*third pencil sketch of character in environment.*

"L" — *Final pencil sketch.*

Acknowledgements

I knew this book would come out well. After all, the subject matter is interesting, the artwork is first-rate, and my friends and I had starring roles. But it probably wouldn't have come out as well as it did without the work of a lot of people who spent way too much time seeing it through.

The book's author, David DeSmith, is someone I know from way back when. Clearly he knew his material and did a pretty decent job of putting the sentences together. Thanks, Dave, I'll see you on the links.

The team at R.J. Reynolds deserves my thanks, too. Martha Burwell, who coordinated the project from the start to finish. Rick Gray, the day-to-day point man; and Don Robertson, the production expert -- each of them busted their humps to get this book done. Without their dedication and talent it never would've made it off the drawing board. To all of them, I am grateful.

I'd also like to thank the gang at Mezzina/Brown, and especially Kerry Kane, John Lee, Mario Marsicano, and Mary Avellino. They might've had the toughest jobs of all, because it was up to them to locate all the artwork. Finding a needle in a haystack is nothing compared to finding an 8-year-old Camel Cash premium illustration.

Last but not least, I'd like to thank the book's designer and publishers. Kathryn Sky-Peck, Peter Ackroyd and Roberta Scimone took all the materials and made it sing. Not only that, they saw to it that the job got done on time. Or almost on time anyway. In addition, their collective editorial and creative contributions are evident throughout the book.

Thanks to all of you. I'm proud of you and of the book. And I'm most proud of the fact that not once during the course of the entire project did I ever have to step in and overrule you! Congratulations on a job well done.

Sincerely,

Photo by Sue Hammerland

David DeSmith is a freelance writer who once worked on the Camel campaign. He now lives with his wife and two sons on Cousins Island, Maine, where he's hard at work on a novel and, when weather permits, his short game.